A JOURNAL OF CONSCIOUSNESS AND TRANSFORMATION

ReVision

CONTENTS

Dancing With Uncertainty

Glenn Aparicio Parry, Jürgen Werner Kremer, Cristina Kaplan, Editors

Cover art "Dancing with Love and Uncertainty" by Joe Cajero,
Acrylic on Canvas, 2014

Winter 2026 • Volume 35 • Number 1

What Is ReVision?

Revisioning, as the name ReVision hints, has been central to the publication's forty year historical trajectory. As our understanding of the leading edge of transformative and consciousness-changing thinking has developed, so has the focus of our mission.

From its origins in humanistic and transpersonal psychologies, ReVision has shifted toward a framework of transdisciplinary, decolonial, and indigenous paradigms. From its origins as an academic journal it has shifted toward a publication which includes art, poetry, story, and articles that translate topics for a broader audience.

With a commitment to the future of humanity and all our relations, ReVision is dedicated to the exploration of issues that assert and value the transmotional and interconnected sovereignty of people before any institutions. Sovereignty and self-determination as foundations of peace require our human imagination as part of a sustainable world of stories and cultural practices in a particular place or ecology.

ReVision welcomes submissions from a wide range of disciplines using a broad spectrum of formats to deepen the process of inquiry, dialogue, and engaged participatory knowing and conversation.

Volume 35, Number 1 (978-1-7362314-4-9)

ReVision (ISSN 0275-6935) is published by
The Society for Indigenous and Ancestral Wisdom and Healing.

Manuscript Submissions

We welcome manuscript submissions.
Manuscript guidelines can be found on our webpage:
http://revisionpublishing.org.

POSTMASTER: Send address changes to
ReVision Publishing,
P.O. Box 1855,
Sebastopol, CA 95473.

Subscriptions

For subscriptions mail a check to above address or go to
www.revisionpublishing.org.

Individual Subscriptions

Subscription for four issues: $44

A sample of articles are available as free access at
revisionpublishing.org

For international subscriptions and orders for individual issues please contact us at
info@revisionpublishing.org

ReVision welcomes dana or donations to support the work of this small nonprofit organization (see revisionpublishing.org).

Please allow six weeks for delivery of first issue.

ReVision Abstracts
Vol. 35 No. 1 • Winter 2026

Baker, Laurelyn, *Wi Wanyang Wacipi* Sundance Lessons. *ReVision, 35(2)*, 26-29. doi:10.4298/REVN.35.2.26-29

Sundancing is a sacred act that has served the author well. Many of the lessons learned, both practical and spiritual, are outlined. Visions from the Sundance have often appeared unexpectedly during stressful times, reenergizing the author to carry on. Her Anishinaabe ancestors have often made important decisions based on visions and dreams that have emanated from the Sundance. The awakenings that have occurred during and after a Sundance are not easy to explain, because a sundance is a liminal space between the worlds, but the magic of a sundance is conveyed as much as possible.

Bickel, M. Poem, *American Silos. ReVision, 35(2)*, 55-63. doi:10.4298/REVN.35.2.55-63

The day after Donald Trump was elected to a second term as president of the United States, the author wrote this poem as a heartfelt effort to make sense of the glaring divide between the political parties and regions of the country–even his next-door neighbor's far-right views. He reaches deep into the historical records of the United States, and of his Northern California region to find and remember the genesis of racist and misogynistic views in the country, and reflects upon them using the extended metaphor of the silo.

Bulkeley, Kelly; Lane Jennifer Marie, Dreams of the US President 2024 *ReVision, 35(2)*, 49-54. doi:10.4298/REVN.35.2.49-54

This article reports on a study of 220 dream reports gathered in a 2024 demographic survey from American adults in response to a question asking if they had ever experienced a dream relating to the election. The reports are sorted and analyzed in terms of seven categories: general dreams about the election, Trump victory, Harris victory, Trump nightmare, Harris nightmare, civil disorder, and encounter with a politician.

Heckel, J. Walking Home in Silence. *ReVision, 35(2)*, 55-63. doi:10.4298/REVN.35.2.55-63

When the author became aware through social media that many of his former high school classmates had become MAGA Republicans, he decided to try to reconnect with them to explore the roots of their current worldviews in their past experiences. However, his approach only met with derision. He explored his disappointment in writing through his regular local newspaper column. A former fraternity brother read the column and messaged him to see if, together, they could try again to form a group. A third fraternity brother joined them to set up a facilitation structure that would allow men with disparate life experiences & viewpoints to talk & listen across differences. The author details their successful meetings over Zoom beginning in 2021, the topics they discussed, the guidelines they adhere to, and, in the men's own words, the positive effects on their lives of the skills that they acquired through participation in the facilitated group process.

Kremer, J. W., There Always Has Been an Alternate Story. *ReVision, 35(2)*, 11-17. doi:10.4298/REVN.35.2.11-17

Indigenous stories of relationality and visionary sovereignty continue to be present the world over. There has always been an alternative to the story of progress that modernity/coloniality continues to perpetrate as its way to control uncertainty. Kent Monkman's painting *Welcoming the Newcomers* is interpreted as a flash of memory, as a material intervention in the work of remembrance of indigenous ways of knowing and being. Attending to this work of remembrance creates the opportunity to transform the winds of delusion the Western Enlightenment traditions have fanned, resulting in our current polycrisis. Exiting the story of modernity/coloniality will bend the moral arc toward justice.

Maroski, L.E., Integrating Perspectives on the Certainty-Uncertainty Paradox. *ReVision, 35(2)*, 4-10. doi:10.4298/REVN.35.2.04-10

This essay explores what I call the certainty-uncertainty paradox through four lenses—philosophical, psychological, sociological, and linguistic. For the philosophical approach, I examine how certainty and uncertainty are often treated as linear opposites separated by degrees of gradation but may be better understood as interdependent and mutually co-arising, each containing the seed of the other. For the psychological approach, I consider the unconscious and conscious dimensions of certainty and uncertainty, and how they manifest in lived experience. At the sociological level, I explore how existential uncertainty—particularly around nuclear weapons and artificial intelligence—emerges from a drive to "win" competitive, finite games of dominance. For the linguistic approach, I examine expressions of un/certainty, including webs of associations and conceptual metaphors that underlie these concepts. I conclude by bringing together the seeming opposites of certainty and uncertainty into a yin/yang-like unity. By becoming aware of the structures of language that maintain our predilection to focus on one part of a complementarity, we can begin not only to realize our responsibilities within the dynamics of Earth and all of her inhabitants, including us, but also to develop new forms of language that reflect our inherent interdependencies and minimize the dissociation of "parts" from the whole of existence.

Parry, Glenn Aparicio, Fascist America or Sacred America: The Choice is Ours. *ReVision, 35(2)*, 39-42. doi:10.4298/REVN.35.2.39-42

This essay contends that the core values of the United States—liberty, equality, and natural rights—were all profoundly influenced by, if not directly appropriated from Native American values, and that Native influence was the primary inspiration for the original founding document that preceded the US Constitution: *The Articles of Confederation*. At the Constitutional Convention, greater power was given to the presidency, and this trend has continued until the present day. The executive branch is now aggressively usurping power from both the legislative and judicial branches, and neither Congress nor the Supreme Court are taking steps to reassert the authority of their own branches. Today's events are not only the continuation of the trend toward greater executive power; they are also the culmination of a half century long effort from the conservative think tank The Heritage Foundation (founded in 1973) to implement a "unitary executive," in which nearly all governmental power would be transferred to the executive branch. If the imbalances in the tripartite government are to be successfully addressed, a second Constitutional convention may need to be convened.

Perkinson, J. W., Facing the Emergent(cy) Future By "Electing" a Different Past. *ReVision, 35(2)*, 18-25. doi:10.4298/REVN.35.2.18-25

The writing here seeks to divine a rhizome: whence the recent election triumph featuring old convictions of white supremacy, Christian nationalism, and male gun adoration, re-tooled to serve tech-billionaire designs on the planet? Sketching Project 2025 agendas as symptomatic of a much older and wider aberration in our species evolution, I will cast an old myth like that of Eden as actually hinting "indigenous" wisdom: a land-articulated limit ("you can harvest from all the trees save one . . ."), disregarded at grave risk of eventual self-destruction. For 5,000 years now, our species has again and again, exceeded local carrying capacity in pushing towards increased numbers and ever more radical extraction and re-engineering of our more-than-human kin. The counter-remedy imagined here (as orientation, not program) is "return"—at least in vision and schooling and appreciation—to what works, indeed, has worked in three million years of history. A re-embrace of values and orientation away from the imperative of rabid growth and "tech possession" to co-creation and mutual flourishing.

Reynolds, Catherine A., A Five-Fold Path of (Re)turning—Weaving the Collective Towards a (Re)turn to Wholeness. *ReVision, 35(2)*, 29-38. doi:10.4298/REVN.35.2.29-38

In the myth of The Old Woman in the Cave, the tapestry of the world is always being made, unmade, and then made again - echoing the constantly changing nature of the Universe. Humanity no longer sees itself as part of nature, no longer remembers what it was to be of the land and not simply on it. Our attempts to conquer and control have resulted in the entire planet now facing perhaps the most chaotic of unravelings we have yet to encounter. Jean Gebser speaks of the structures of consciousness humanity has experienced in his book The Ever-Present Origin. We are being called now to shift our collective consciousness once more; to remember the languages our bodies and hearts once knew, to listen to and speak with the Earth and return to our origin with Nature. Walking the five- fold path laid out in this work is one of the ways we might begin to embrace the collective uncertainty. Through practices focused on partnerships, plants, place and pith (the thread that ties us all together) we can begin to remember the old stories and listen to the voices of those we once called kin.

Scott, Barbara (Be), The Living Heart of the Constitution. *ReVision, 35(2)*, 43-48. doi:10.4298/REVN.35.2.43-48

This article begins with the experience of a group of acquaintances in Taos, New Mexico, who began meeting a week after the November 5 election, in which Donald Trump defeated Kamala Harris. The organizer of the group (the author) sensed that one of the most useful ways to reclaim truth from the jaws of propaganda would be to share it with one another in small groups that might meet regularly and expand their reach. The purpose was and still is to build community and keep open the lines of sincere, civil communication, with the hope that each person could extrapolate these trust-inducing methods into their own sphere of self-respect and respect for others. The article then interleaves the group's experience with a history of the Constitution, in particular the Preamble and its author, Gouverneur Morris, who was selected to give the Constitution its final language. In the process, he entirely rewrote the Preamble to emphasize unity over individualism, which this author argues became a "coiled spring of vision" that will never be uncoiled in the hearts of Americans who have repeatedly heard the words and consider them their rightful legacy.

Created by the United Nations General Assembly in 1980, the University for Peace trains future leaders to explore and formulate strategies and practices to address the causes of problems affecting human and global wellbeing.

The MA and PhD Degree in Indigenous Science and Peace Studies (ISPS)

This program examines the traditions of Indigenous peoples of the world and their generations-tested ways of making peace and balancing societies, offering a roadmap to prosperity that respects individual and collective rights, local development models and environmental solutions.

IS IT FOR YOU?

Do you want to help solve the global crises facing humanity by transforming outdated paradigms?

Are you inspired to learn how Indigenous knowledge and Western science can be employed across disciplines and professions to transform crises and conflicts, and build peace?

Do you want to spend a year studying in an academically challenging environment, at a global university with students, faculty, and Indigenous Elders from around the world?

WHAT WILL YOU LEARN?

Steeped in Indigenous Knowledge Systems and methodologies, the MA or PhD Degree in Indigenous Science and Peace Studies (ISPS) will train you to be an insightful researcher and practitioner who understands the central issues that impact diplomacy, policymaking, and community work.

Learn a synthesis of indigenous scientific research and theory relevant to the transformation of conflicts.

Gain a diversity of perspectives that impact peace, justice, security, sovereignty, and reconciliation.

Obtain detailed knowledge of the United Nations System and related institutions, procedures and instruments that affect decision-making regarding Indigenous peoples and traditional knowledge.

This course enables students to become more effective policymakers, community workers, diplomats, activists, and communicators who create change to renew life on earth.

**For more information, go to https://isri.wisn.org.
To apply, go to www.upeace.org/pages/apply-admission.**

The main campus of the University for Peace is located in San Jose, Costa Rica

Editors' Introduction

Glenn Aparicio Parry
Jürgen Werner Kremer
Cristina Kaplan

There is the old Chinese story about a farmer who buys a horse that then runs away. A neighbor remarks, "That's bad news." The farmer replies, "Good news, bad news, who can say?" The horse returns and brings along another horse. The farmer gives the second horse to his son, who rides it, but then badly breaks his leg. Everyone is consoling the farmer about the bad news, but he again says, "Good news, bad news, who can tell." And sure enough, the emperor's men come and take every able-bodied young man to fight in a war, but the farmer's son is spared.

This story illustrates the uncertainty inherent in life. *Dancing with Uncertainty*, the title of this issue, was originally the title for a conference held in the summer of 2020 at the start of the worldwide pandemic. The Covid-19 pandemic may be behind us, but in 2024 we were faced with an unexpected return of Mr. Trump to the White House. His relentless political actions, often erratic, if somewhat predictable (since based on Project 2025), have engendered anew a feeling of uncertainty, if not dread among many people in the U.S. and throughout the world. The current quality of uncertainty is distinct from the fundamental existential threat created by the coronavirus. Human agency looms much larger in the current political climate of uncertainty. Suddenly, the viability of the United States as a democratic republic is in question, as is the state of the entire world that seemed more predictable even just a few years ago.

This issue delves below the surface of contemporary political events to examine some of the root causes of instability in the world today. We explore a host of issues regarding uncertainty, from holding paradox and the integrity of opposites, to the stories and mythologies behind disruptions and chaos together with the possible good that can come out of it, to the promise and pitfalls of democratic republics and the visionary sovereignty of Native America that influenced the founding fathers of the United States.

L. E. Maroski delves deep into the heart of the certainty/uncertainty paradox, bringing terms that seem to be opposites together in a way that highlight their independence as well as their interdependence, and even their mutual co-arising. She briefly explores philosophical, psychological, sociological, and linguistic approaches, understanding that each approach offers a different type of map that enables us to see different aspects of the territory. She creates novel structures, not just neologisms, not as a synthesis, but as a lens to view complementarities as one.

Jürgen W. Kremer reminds us, whatever the overpowering forces of the modern West, the alternate stories of Indigenous provenance have always persisted. The originally empowering winds of the European Enlightenment traditions have presently turned into winds of delusion as we have entered the dead-end-street of the present polycrisis. The ongoing erasure of Indigenous traditions the world over highlights the suicidality of the Western model of progress. Kremer asserts that our primary challenge is not one of progress in any form, but of the need to change the story that we are acting in—from addictive obsession with progress and development to one of relationality, care, and balancing ourselves within the web of life. An interpretation of Kent Monkman's monumental painting *Welcoming the Newcomers,* created for the Metropolitan Museum of Art in New York City, highlights the pluriversal worlds it depicts and the potential of reversals and remembrances. It evokes the continuation of alternate stories of visionary sovereignty embodied in Indigenous paradigms. The algorithms of stories, ceremonies, and place facilitate the emergence of grounded hope in the face of uncertainty.

James W. Perkinson discusses white supremacy, Christian nationalism, and male gun adoration as symptoms of an older aberration in our species evolution. He points to the indigenous roots that we all carry, the indigenous wisdom that is available to all of us. Disregarding this wisdom puts us in danger of self-destruction. He calls for a return to ancient knowledge that has worked for millions of years as remedy for our current polycrisis, our "rabid growth and 'tech possession'".

Laurelyn Baker, an Anishinaabe Sundancer, introduces a different perspective on dancing with uncertainty, asserting that sundancing is a creative, liminal space between the worlds. She chronicles some of the spiritual insights she gained as a sundancer, insights that have enabled her to face the challenges of today with equanimity and a sense of humor.

Catherine (Cat) Reynolds begins with an overarching myth of an old woman making a beautiful weaving who is then interrupted by a trickster figure that unravels her creation. In Native cultures, the trickster is generally accepted as a part of creation; everything emerges and returns to the flux and nothing is perfectly finished. She goes on to address the sacred way of tea and other perennial wisdom that must be remembered and reintegrated into modern knowledge if humanity is to survive and thrive. Such wisdom acknowledges kinship with the more-than-human world.

Glenn Aparicio Parry's piece unveils the roots of uncertain leadership in today's US politics. He chronicles how we began as far away from monarchy as possible with a system closely modeled after tribal government; yet since the Constitutional convention we have been gravitating toward ceding more and more power to the presidency. The second Trump presidency is the culmination of this trend, dangerously shifting the balance of power to the executive branch. Parry concludes that a second Constitutional convention is necessary if we are to correct the imbalances within our current tripartite government.

Be Scott puts the onus on *We the People* for rebalancing our system of government. "Crossing her own Delaware to protect the Constitution and its Bill of Rights," she formed a "heartwarming" support group after the 2024 presidential election that has been meeting ever since. Her concept is to embrace the essence of democratic government, building community from the grass roots level. Her piece includes a fascinating look at Gouverneur Morris, a little-known historical figure who took a leadership role in crafting the Preamble to the Constitution.

Kelly Bulkeley and Jennifer Marie Lane discuss their analysis of 220 dreams gathered in 2024. It shows that the meaning of dreams extends beyond the personal sphere of individuals to social experiences and collective concerns. They find that people's dreams of a politician represent a measure of the politician's charisma. Their analysis shows that politically-themed dreaming appears to be distributed across the ideological spectrum.

John Heckel and Michael Bickford explore the difficulty of dialoguing across our current political divides. John facilitated a zoom group consisting of people with disparate life experiences and political viewpoints. This contribution is a creative braiding of facilitator reflections, participant statements, and poetry. It is a powerful illustration of how such a potentially hazardous dialogue can be facilitated

As the Chinese story of the farmer illustrates, uncertainty is an inevitable part of life. Quantum theories suggest an alert beyond this fundamental existential predicament by emphasizing the role of the observer in the arising of reality. If reality is indeed observer dependent, then the measurements, intentions, and ethics of the observer become an important issue: we as humans hold an important responsibility in our co-creative intra-actions. Our observational process is implicated and we need to be acutely aware of the ethico-ontoepistemological lens we are holding. Which paradigm are we in? Which story are we a part of? What is our responsibility to the web of relationality we are embedded in? Which framework are we using to respond to uncertainty? How do we dance, think, envision, story, and relate to each other? The articles of this issue may help to sharpen the depth of our self-reflection and ethical engagement with the worlds we are creating.

Our Cover Image

Dancing with Love and Uncertainty (2014)—Joe Cajero

The painting shows the dance of the masculine and feminine, femininity on the right and masculinity on the left. Two Spirits are symbolized by the two stars and the presence of the Creator symbolized by the Moon. The surface of the Mother Earth is symbolized by yellow crust and greenery. The plant on the left symbolizes the natural intelligence of all living things to grow; the three leaves at the top symbolize body, mind and spirit.

The center of the painting represents the flux of creation, a transition of darkness into the light, emerging out of the formless void into manifestation. With hope, faith and love, it is here where the whole of creation, both feminine and masculine, dances with uncertainty.

Integrating Perspectives on the Certainty-Uncertainty Paradox

L.E. Maroski

"The more uncertain I have felt about myself, the more there has grown up in me a feeling of kinship with all things."
–Carl Jung, *Memories, Dreams, Reflections*

Although our present era seems particularly fraught with uncertainty, every time in history has had its uncertainties, sometimes regarding whether the harvest will be sufficient for the winter, sometimes regarding worldwide political instability. Our time is no different, and our time is unique. Not only is there uncertainty at the scale of society, but each person has likely felt greater uncertainty about something in their life recently. Although uncertainty is a ubiquitous experience, why does it seem so overwhelming now, and how can we manage our response to it?

In the quote from Jung, above, an initial interpretation seems to be that feeling certain of one's identity separates one from others, but when such an ego boundary is more porous, it is possible to feel interconnected and perhaps even question where one's boundaries end and those of others begin. Uncertainty, not about external circumstances but about one's self, could have profound effects. Such questioning could lead one to a deeper interpenetration of uncertainty and certainty and self and other, as well as other seemingly separate concepts that co-arise interdependently.

We will mostly take up "unsureness," but the other meanings make cameo appearances. By referring to a "certainty-uncertainty paradox," I am not synthesizing them into a new unity (as with "bittersweet") but rather bringing terms that seem to be opposites together in a way that highlights their independence as well as their interdependence, even their mutual co-arising. By recognizing that at the core of certainty is uncer-

> By recognizing that at the core of certainty is uncertainty, and at the core of uncertainty is certainty, it might be possible to reframe one's experiences.

The term "paradox" comes from the Greek *para* meaning "contrary to" and *doxa*, opinion (from *dokein*, "to appear, seem, think"). It came to refer to self-contradictory statements in the 1560s. Some philosophers believe that paradoxes emerged from early Greek riddles (Quine, 1976). Although English has only one word, uncertainty, German has three words that convey its different valences: *ungenauigkeit*, inexactness; *unsicherheit*, unsureness; and *unbestimmtheit*, unascertainable, indeterminable.

tainty, and at the core of uncertainty is certainty, it might be possible to reframe one's experiences.

It was probably no coincidence that after I accepted the request to write this article—when my life was quite stable and I silently wondered how I could say anything about uncertainty—the new administration in the U.S. arrived and threw my life into significant uncertainty. In light of the promised cuts of government staff I feared that I would lose my job. Because I was a contractor,

L.E. (Lisa) Maroski blends philosophy, psychology, and science with the spiritual to describe her vision for a new type of language and to provide stepping stones for possible ways to express the paradoxical wholeness of Life. In *Embracing Paradox, Evolving Language,* her words ring out as a clarion call to visionaries who seek to bring into existence a world of many worlds that works for everybody.

I assumed that contractors would be let go first, given the protections in place for federal employees. My fear was augmented when, one Monday morning, I logged on and got an "Access Denied" message. None of the Information Technology people I contacted could help me restore access. The next day I learned, not from my supervisor but from friends, that government employees were given a buyout package. As a contractor, I got no such thing. What did that mean? Would I now have to pick up the slack left by federal employees who took the bait? I didn't know whether I would have any work or too much work.

Despite such experience of high uncertainty, fortunately, it was not radical uncertainty. I do not need to doubt the basis of my existence. I do not doubt that my computer will continue to run, water will flow from the tap, and I will be able to get this article written. Certainties in those domains helped to balance out the uncertainty in my employment domain. My sense of self—who I am and what I stand for—has, ironically, been clarified and solidified.

Because *feelings* of uncertainty are highly subjective and can involve internal, visceral clenching (which is how my body reacts to uncertainty), let us first look at how others have approached the concept of un/certainty, in order to establish some common ground and thereby also *understand* un/certainty. Doing so will reveal tools, perspectives, and approaches that take us beyond the visceral level.

We will briefly explore philosophical, psychological, sociological, and linguistic approaches to certainty and uncertainty. Each approach is like a different type of map that enables us to see different aspects of the territory. Philosophy gives us the broad contours, both topological and conceptual. Psychology provides details about the surface and deep terrain, including how we experience the tension between certainty and uncertainty, either in the concepts themselves or as they affect other aspects of lived experience. A sociological lens enables us to look at how we navigate together through collective uncertainties regarding our continued existence on Earth. And finally, after traversing and examining those lenses through which we experience the terrain of un/certainty, we will look at how our language itself filters and shapes our perceptions so that we can begin to envision new ways to get beyond the exclusion of certainty from uncertainty, and vice versa, to be able to express and embody their paradoxical nature.

Philosophical Approach

The concepts of certainty and uncertainty are related to each other in various ways—most commonly, as linear opposites separated by degrees of gradation. As distinct concepts, certainty is not uncertainty; indeed, one seems to be the negation of the other. Of course, it is not as simple as that.

The fundamental question at the core of both certainty and uncertainty is "what do I know that I know?" What I know I know (think I know, believe I know) is called epistemic certainty. I know basic mathematics, such that I am certain that $2 + 5 = 7$, not only from rote memorization but also from experiences of adding objects or money. Epistemic certainty also includes what I know that I don't know, such as how to distinguish edible from poisonous wild mushrooms. In this manner, the un/sureness valence of un/certainty functions as an overtone to our knowledge or beliefs that reflects a self-evaluation that is layered onto the content of the knowledge or belief. Another metaphor: this type of un/certainty is like the readout of a reliability meter applied to knowledge. But what gives that readout credence?

Epistemic certainty does not encompass the actuality of whether your knowledge is true or accurate. If you have ever tried to put something together without reading the instructions, then gotten stuck, you had high epistemic certainty without it necessarily corresponding to accurate knowledge. Epistemic certainty can always be questioned and thereby refined by a healthy dose of skepticism—is this the whole picture? How do I know this? Might there be more to learn about this?

The limitations of our knowledge are a function of the limitations of our perspective. For a simple example, consider that you are shown an object, like this.

If this were all you saw and you had no other previous experience with such objects, you might insist it does not have a handle. The converse would be true for the object below: you would say that it most certainly does have a handle.

These examples using a coffee mug are metaphoric for how we can or cannot know another's experience. In other words, we cannot be certain that our experience of something corresponds to others' experiences. Therefore, it is prudent to seek out perspectives other than those most familiar to us.

In contrast to epistemic certainty, epistemic *uncertainty* is more difficult to characterize because it is related not just to lack of knowledge but also to doubt and to one's inability to predict or possibly even imagine the future. As the government firings began, for example, it was difficult to predict where the DOGE (Department of Government Efficiency) team would strike next. Eventually a pattern emerged (they first dismantled agencies that Elon Musk had a beef with), but then the pattern changed, and even agencies essential for national security were hit. Americans had to face the uncertainty of what life would be like without a government that could perform important governmental functions, including ensuring safety and security.

One could metaphorically characterize epistemic uncertainty as a field from which certainties arise temporarily, like waves forming on the surface of the ocean but then subsiding back into it [John Dotson, personal communication]. However, as Werner Heisenberg's famous uncertainty principle reveals, there is a limit to what we can know precisely—the more precisely we know the location of a particle the less we can simultaneously know about its momentum. That which we cannot know, called aleatory uncertainty, locks us out of omniscience.

One factor that keeps uncertainty from being overridden by the fantasy of certainty is the seeming randomness or stochasticity of events—from living within an open system to the unintended consequences of our actions, to the reactions of others, to our limited perspectivity. Terry Gilliam's dystopian movie *Brazil*, for example, illustrates a completely unforeseen unfolding of events from the random occurrence of a fly falling into a typewriter. We each have less dramatic examples of such uncertainty happening every day of our lives.

The philosopher Ludwig Wittgenstein challenged the notion of certainty and uncertainty as linear opposites, offering instead a more complex, nonlinear relationship between them. In *On Certainty*, he wrote about what can be doubted (Wittgenstein, 1972). Can the ability to doubt be doubted? In asking that question, he realized that doubting relies on certain things that cannot themselves be doubted, such as the meanings of the very words used to express the doubt. Thus, he recognized that the intentional uncertainty of doubting *presupposes and depends on* the very certainty it attempts to undermine. Otherwise, you find yourself in an infinite regression of doubt. That infinite regress does not result in any knowledge or certainty. Rather, it shows that the relationship between certainty and uncertainty is not a linear opposition but more like a yin-yang rela-tionship in which certainty is at the core of uncertainty and uncertainty at the core of certainty. By doubting un/certainty, you learn something about your relationship to the fact or proposition that you are doubting, not something new about the fact or proposition itself; for example, you realize what you value or what you assume to be true.

Epistemic certainty can be imitated albeit falsely when belief is substituted for knowing. To be overly certain of one's beliefs, however, can be a form of addiction and/or a form of psychopathy. Although there is a natural tension *between* certainty and uncertainty, when the tension *within* uncertainty becomes unbearable, that is, when one cannot face truth to resolve the tension, it can be tempting to believe one's own lies in order to maintain (a false) "certainty." (One's reliability meter malfunctions.) The movie *Sunset Boulevard* shows this: an aging movie star cannot face the fact that she is a "has been." She needs to be certain that her fans still adore her. Her butler helps to feed that delusion. In this case, she has succumbed to a pathology called pseudologia phantastica, in which one believes one's own lies, not necessarily to intentionally deceive others but because one can maintain a conscious feeling of certainty only by deceiving oneself. Thus, ontological un/certainty, which philosophers deal with, differs from psychological un/certainty.

Psychological Approach

It is possible to see the importance of a nondual understanding of certainty-uncertainty by applying an analytical psychological lens, in particular, by examining the unconscious and conscious dimensions of certainty and uncertainty and how they manifest in lived experience. Let's consider the combinations of conscious and unconscious awareness with certainty and uncertainty.

First, consider the conscious dimension. This dimension is readily available to awareness, especially when attention is directed to it. Conscious certainty includes many of the "givens" of life as dictated by one's culture—e.g., that the sun will rise, the electric bill will come due, and that someday each of us will die. Often, however, conscious certainty does not feel like certainty because the element of choice or of judgment is gone. It occurs as "what's so" or what "just is." It is in the "isness" that the certainty resides, unquestioned and sometimes unquestionable. Conscious certainty can also be experienced as a self-perceived ability to predict an outcome or a future occurrence and conscious uncertainty as the inability to predict the future.

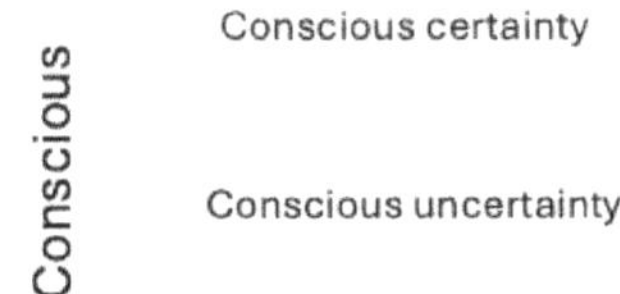

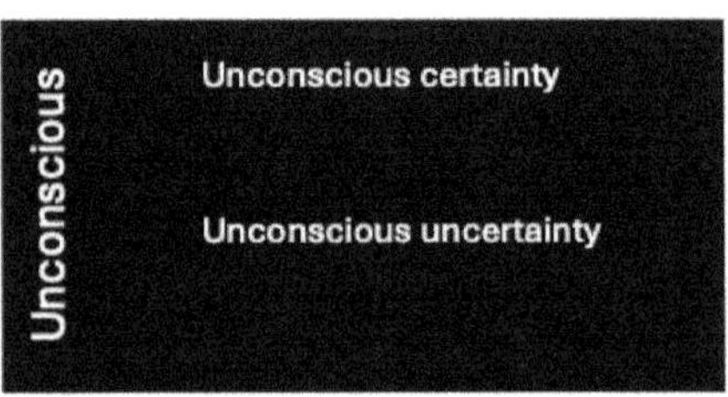

Conscious uncertainty can arouse fear and its downstream emotions, such as anger, anxiety, and catastrophizing, specifically when one knows that one currently has such emotions. In the example from my own life, I am very conscious of the uncertainties regarding my employment. In other domains, conscious uncertainty looks like this: he loves me; he loves me not? Is the snowstorm going to delay the flight? Rarely do we consciously confront uncertainties such as, "do I exist?"

For many indigenous cultures that co-create the rising of the sun or do not have a sense of conscious certainty about events such as the sun rising each day (perhaps a volcanic eruption that blocked the sun for months in the past resulted in culturally created conscious uncertainty), rituals were developed to ensure (i.e., transform conscious uncertainty toward conscious certainty—but not completely otherwise the ritual would be pointless) that the sun will rise again tomorrow, that rain will come, and so on. Currently, many of us in the U.S. are facing high levels of conscious uncertainty about whether we will receive Social Security checks in our retirement, whether our democratic system of government will devolve into total authoritarianism, and whether climate chaos will be able to be reversed or at least abated.

The forms of unconscious certainty and uncertainty are harder to recognize, particularly in oneself, although they might be more evident in others. Although Wittgenstein did not use the psychological language of conscious and unconscious, he recognized that foundational certainties operate unconsciously and make conscious uncertainty or doubt possible. Unconscious certainty involves beliefs that are taken for granted at a more fundamental level than conscious certainty. For example, when you walk across your living room floor, as you have done thousands of times already, you have developed an unconscious certainty that the floor won't dematerialize and that your foot will be supported by it. Such object permanence developed through experiences that confirm and reinforce each other. Similarly, we develop event predictability through calendrical regularities, such as birthdays and holidays, which allow life to feel more stable and knowable, thereby reducing some it its inherent uncertainty.

Unconscious uncertainty truly is unconscious. It might not manifest as our usual feelings and anxieties of conscious uncertainty. In fact, conscious certainties can hide unconscious uncertainties, resulting in cognitive-emotional dissonance. "For example, a mother may be incapable of giving up the belief that her son did not commit a gruesome murder, and yet, compatible with that inextinguishable belief, she may be tortured by doubt" (Reed, 2022). Unconscious uncertainty can also be seen in complexes or pathological responses that erupt when conscious certainty is used unconsciously as a shield to protect oneself from experiencing conscious uncertainty. For example, unconscious uncertainty can manifest as irrational fears that emerge unexpectedly, displacing the original uncertainty onto something that can be faced consciously. One member of a couple, for example, might deflect their unconscious uncertainty about their spouse's fidelity by projecting onto their adolescent child a conscious "certainty" (not necessarily accurate) that the adolescent is being promiscuous. Such projection enables the unconscious uncertainty about the spouse's fidelity to remain hidden and unexamined.

At the same time, it surfaces the anger associated with infidelity but redirects it toward the wrong person, often someone more vulnerable. Similar projections of unconscious uncertainty happen at the societal level, when uncertainty about one's social standing is intensified by actions of the owner class (e.g., by outsourcing jobs overseas) but projected onto those of lower social standing, such as immigrants.

Sociological Approach

When humans developed the capacity to destroy the earth with nuclear bombs, the collective unconscious certainty that the infinite game—life on Earth—would continue indefinitely gave way to widespread conscious uncertainty about our fate—"our" including all species on Earth. (James Carse [1986] defined finite games as those meant to be won/lost, such as sporting events and elections, in contrast to infinite games which are played so that the game can continue to be played ad infinitum; life is considered an infinite game, as is democracy. Democracy can continue indefinitely because it has finite games—elections—embedded within it.) The finite, win-lose nuclear war games of humans threatens our own foundation—namely, if Earth is destroyed then both the finite games and the infinite game here cease (Carse, 1986).

In an illustrative case of life imitating art, or as with Werner Heisenberg, life imitating science, Heisenberg introduced the term "uncertainty" into physics with a specific technical meaning relating to the "simultaneous measurement of canonically conjugate variables, such as position and momentum, or energy and time" (Frayn, 2010, p. 98). He also recognized the conjugate nature of certainty and uncertainty: the more precisely you measure one variable, the less precise your measurement of the related variable can be; and this ratio, the uncertainty relationship, is itself precisely formulable" (Frayn, 2010, p. 98). Heisenberg, the head of the German nuclear program during WWII, struggled with his own moral uncertainty as to what to do with the knowledge that gave him the capability to develop nuclear weapons. If he developed them for Hitler, he might help his own country win the war, but he also knew that Hitler might use them in horrific ways. Heisenberg was caught in the tension of different, competing contexts—on the one hand, he worked for the Nazis yet he also wanted to distance himself from them and their ideology, particularly their condemnation of "Jewish physics," which was essentially the type of physics he was doing. He also did not want to be perceived as a traitor. He did not want his country to think he had lost them the war intentionally nor did he want them to think they lost due to his incompetence. To what extent he was conscious of those conflicting motivations is not known for sure, as biographers have struggled to determine, with certainty, whether Heisenberg intentionally slowed the German nuclear program.

In contrast, the Americans developed nuclear weapons from the conscious certainty that Hitler and his fascist regime had to be stopped. At the same time, they grappled with uncertainties—perhaps conscious, perhaps unconscious—about whether the atom bomb would ignite the atmosphere and destroy life on Earth. I am not condoning the use of nuclear weapons, only showing what we humans do when faced with conscious certainty and uncertainty. Today we face a similar situation regarding artificial intelligence.

Even while the nuclear threat still looms, we have added more types of threats to the continuation of the game of life, including our disrupting of Earth's homeodynamic processes (often called

> The forms of unconscious certainty and uncertainty are harder to recognize, particularly in oneself, although they might be more evident in others.

climate change) as well as the deployment of automated learning systems (artificial general intelligence, AGI) that have already figured out how to lie and manipulate us. The long-term consequences of continuing to develop AGI are not known, but the developers are certain that they must continue the AGI race just so that the opposition (whether another company or another country) doesn't win this self-defined game. Just as nuclear weapons were developed to win the war—without regard to the consequences of nuclear radiation and fallout—AGI is being developed just to win a finite game that could, ironically, end the role of humans in the infinite game of life.

As a society we also now must deal with a new type of epistemic uncertainty in the form of mass-produced, intentionally spread misinformation (lies spread unconsciously) and disinformation (lies spread consciously, with intent to deceive or manipulate). Many previously authoritative (i.e., trustworthy) sources of information have been undermined, sometimes from within, often from without. There is now public gaslighting as well as blatant mendacity across the media spectrum. Who can we trust when it is becoming increasingly clear that no one sees the whole picture, as the mug example above illustrates?

Linguistic Approach

Because our understanding and experience of un/certainty occurs via language, I will also examine linguistic expressions of un/certainty, including their webs of associations, as well as the conceptual metaphors that underlie these concepts. I then propose ways to bring together these "opposites" into a yin/yang-like unity.

We express our certainty and uncertainty by using language. Language is more than just words and their etymologies. Words/concepts are related to other concepts through webs of associations conditioned not only by derivation but also by use. Such webs are unique to each individual, but likely there are many overlaps among people who share a culture. Wittgenstein, in *Philosophical Investigations,* claimed that words/concepts do not have an essence but they do show family resemblances (Wittgen-

stein & Anscombe, 1958). Further, we know what a word means by how it is used. The figure below shows my web of associations for the pair "certainty-uncertainty."

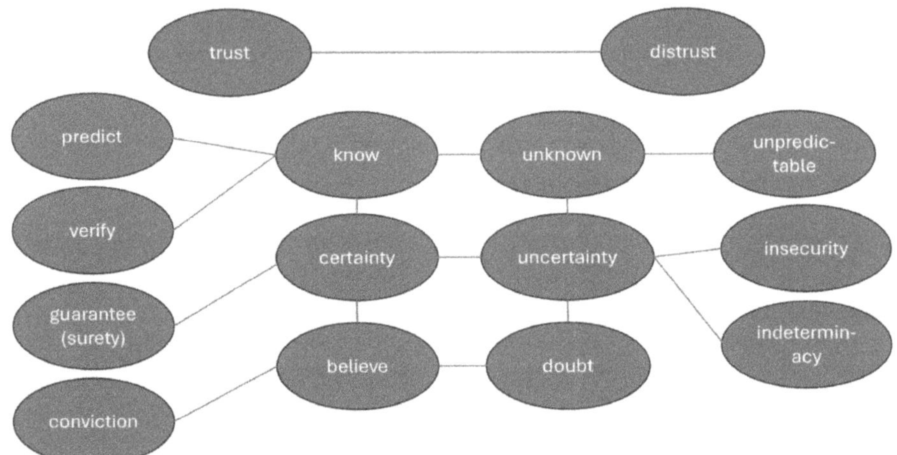

As you can see, the terms certainty and uncertainty also call to mind other pairs of concepts, such as believe-doubt, trust-distrust. This example of a web of associations is relatively abstract; it doesn't include specifics about what I know, believe, whom I trust to have reliable information, and so on. Those particulars would also be part of each person's web of associations. It is in those very details that our ability to communicate has been breaking down. Some of us would put conspiracy theorists on the "trust/certainty" side of the web

un/certainty directly, so such webs also include the less formal expressions we use, such as, "I think that...; I know that...; I have no idea whether...; I might have...; do you suppose that...; and your guess is as good as mine." *Waiting for Godot* is an ode to uncertainty.

Underlying our everyday discourse about un/certainty is a largely unconscious system of metaphors that we use not only to express such concepts but also to reason about them. Such conceptual metaphors were identified by George Lakoff and Mark Johnson in a groundbreaking book called *Metaphors We Live By* (Lakoff & Johnson, 2008). Certainty is often expressed by metaphors of solidity (foundation, rock, ground), is characterized as an object or property that

> If certainty is at the core of uncertainty, is it possible not just to become conscious of the certainty at the heart of uncertainty and the uncertainty at the core of certainty, but to be able to access the opposites together and the psychic energy that the tension between them provides?

while others would put legacy media on the "trust/certainty" side. Some wouldn't know where to put those sources of information. Given that type of meta-uncertainty, it is understandable that people are uncertain about how to deal with their uncertainty.

In English, we tend not to express

someone or something (e.g., knowledge) can have, and is good (up, high, moral). Conversely, uncertainty is characterized by risk, chance (gambling), and by terms such as "undermine" which convey the removal of firm foundations. These metaphoric associations also fit into the web of associations.

Those types of implicit metaphors that underlie our literal language unconsciously influence how we think about things and reason about solving problems. Similarly, moral certainty often derives from one's subjective rationality, which then is used to justify behavior. For example, if it is argued that crime is a beast, it would be rational to want to kill such a beast, eliminate the threat it poses, eradicate it, and so on. Conversely, if one believes that crime is a virus, it would be rational to pursue methods to heal those afflicted (Thibodeau & Boroditsky, 2011). Thus, the metaphoric framing that we use to define problems influences how we reason about solving them. Indeed, we see vast differences in cultures, whether criminals are imprisoned or whether methods of reconciliation or restitution are used. Thus, sometimes certainty is only as deep as the metaphors used to characterize a situation.

How can we more consciously utilize language in the dance of certainty and uncertainty? Our dancing with them must involve more than simply shifting from one foot to the other. Trying to stand on both feet simultaneously effectively stops the dancing. Perhaps the dance involves stepping out of such an either/or mindset.

Indeed, Wittgenstein pointed the way when he realized that we necessarily rely on some things to remain certain while engaging in intentional uncertainty (i.e., philosophical doubt) (Wittgenstein, 1972). As yin is at the heart of yang, and vice versa, his ideas suggest that certainty is at the heart of uncertainty.

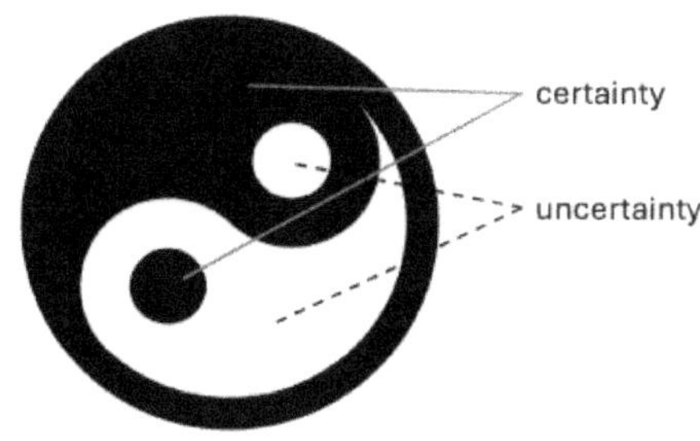

Even as we express uncertainty in language, it is necessary to assume some certainty that the words one uses can and will be understood by others—that we have sufficient shared agreement about their meanings. We can look not just to the words for certainty but also to the grammar—i.e., aspects of language that tell us what must be expressed. For example, some languages require speakers to indicate grammatically *how* it is they know something. These syntactic

> By looking for the certainties at the heart of the uncertainties we face, not only can we circumvent a vicious downward cycle, but we can find some solidity with which to anchor ourselves to weather the storms of uncertainty then rebuild life, society, and hope.

elements are called evidentials. English does not have syntactic evidentials, but when necessary we can (but are not required to) specify how we know, for example, that "there was a cougar nearby." We could express it using different sentence constructions, depending on whether the knowledge was first-hand ("I saw the cougar"), through signs ("I saw cougar footprints by the river," or, these days "my neighbor's doorbell camera showed footage of a cougar on their porch"), or from hearsay ("Uncle Bob told me that he saw a cougar"). Evidentials provide a rough indication on the "reliability meter" of certainty. Consider how different social media would be if we were required grammatically to assert that your re-post is simply hearsay.

If certainty is at the core of uncertainty, is it possible not just to become conscious of the certainty at the heart of uncertainty and the uncertainty at the core of certainty, but to be able to access the opposites together and the psychic energy that the tension between them provides?

To return to my situation as an example, my uncertainty lies initially in the fear that I might lose my job and the subsequent cascade of further unknowns that I would have to consider if I did lose my job—for example, will I be able to afford to continue living here if I lose my job; what do I want to do with my life now? In addition to such personal unknowns, we are facing similar uncer-

tainties at a societal level. For example, what if the government collapses because there aren't enough people left to keep it functioning minimally; do we still have enough trust in our fellow humans to help each other out during these crises?

You probably noticed that I combined certainty and uncertainty into one word by writing "un/certainty" to convey both simultaneously. It is convenient to do that with terms that are spelled similarly. However, it would not work as well for complementarities of different words, such as "self" and "other," to write them as "un/self" or even "self/other." Thus, to continue to engage interdependent concepts simultaneously, we will need to develop novel ways to express them— and I do mean novel structures, not just neologisms (Maroski, 2024). A structure such as *(self/others)* reminds the reader that self and others are not opposite ends of a continuum but are interdependent aspects of a greater reality, that each one of us, as a seemingly separate self, relies on others not simply for comfort, services, etc, but to give us a sense of self in the first place. If there were no others, there would be no self. And the dance is ongoing, a process, not a static thing or state.

Relationships like that of certainty and uncertainty, in which one concept is at the heart of the other, can be characterized by a new type of relationship category, which I call *fu-an-gu*, a glyph I invented for a science-philosophy novel to convey paradoxes of the following type: "the deeper you go, the less it looks like itself; and when you reach the core, it looks like the opposite of what you started with" (Maroski, 2024). Wittgenstein looked deeply into doubt and found that it required certainty. Physicists looked deeply into matter and found energy.

It is my hope that by becoming aware of the structures of language that maintain our predilection to focus on one part of a complementarity (such as "uncertainty" or "conscious" or "self"), we can begin not only to realize our responsibilities within the dynamics of Earth and all of her inhabitants, including us, but also to develop new forms of language that reflect our inherent interdependencies and minimize the dissociation of "parts" from the whole of existence. In addition, by acknowledging the interdependence of concepts such as certainty and uncertainty, we gain a more insightful and constructive lens for navigating the vagaries of life. By looking for the certainties at the heart of the uncertainties we face, not only can we circumvent a vicious downward cycle, but we can find some solidity with which to anchor ourselves to weather the storms of uncertainty and begin to rebuild life, society, and hope.

And, while writing this article, I did lose my job in the DOGE cuts. I have no idea how I will earn money in the future, but I am certain, and committed, that it will be by bringing forth these ideas about language and paradox into the world.

References

Carse, J. P. (1986). *Finite and Infinite Games*. New York: Free Press.

Frayn, M. (2010). *Copenhagen*: Knopf Doubleday Publishing Group.

Lakoff, G., & Johnson, M. (2008). *Metaphors We Live By*: University of Chicago Press.

Maroski, L. E. (2024). *Embracing Paradox, Evolving Language: Expressing the Unity and Complexity of Integral Consciousness*. Longmont, CO: Untimely Books.

Quine, W. V. (1976). *The Ways of Paradox, and Other Essays*: Harvard University Press.

Reed, B. (2022). Certainty. In E. N. Zalta (Ed.), *The Stanford Encyclopedia of Philosophy*.

Thibodeau, P. H., & Boroditsky, L. (2011). The Role of Metaphor in Reasoning. *PLOS ONE*, 6(2), e16782.

Wittgenstein, L. (1972). *On Certainty*: HarperCollins.

Wittgenstein, L., & Anscombe, G. E. M. (1958). *Philosophical Investigations: The English Text of the Third Edition*: Prentice Hall.

The Prophecy of the Eagle and Condor, 1993. Mazatl Galindo.

There Always Has Been an Alternate Story

Jürgen Werner Kremer

With the beginnings of European enlightenment traditions, a new mental current started to arise. In the beginning its winds carried the bright light that dispersed church dogmata unable to withstand its revelatory scientific investigations. Yet, as these winds blew across time, the light it carried darkened and phantoms began to inhabit its currents. The winds of enlightenment increasingly became dark winds of delusion. The dance with uncertainty changed from a dance of grounded hope to an obsession with the control of the material world and the insistence on the increasing powers of control as Western science and technology developed together with what today have become neoliberal forms of politics and economy.

The phantoms inhabiting these powerful currents were born from a significant, and seemingly benign, move of consciousness. Their phantasmagorical birth is the culmination of a long process on European lands. The rejection of church dogma and the assertion of free and critical inquiry enabled two interrelated processes: 1) The development of a powerful materialistic and reduction-

1995, 2011; Mignolo & Walsh, 2018), the two Siamese twins that to this day continue their global destructive impact.

Uncertainty is an inevitable part of life (unpredictable weather, unpredictable harvests, etc.); and uncertainty is also the companion of free will, choice, and imagination—while we have control over our intentions we do not have control over the results. Uncertainty is

> The normative dissociation of Westernized minds relegated what is intimately woven into Indigenous minds to the world of phantoms.

ist metaphysics that continues to facilitate so many contemporary benefits by way of its emphasis on empirical data together with the resulting technological boons. 2) Intertwined with it is the vanquishing of an Indigenous pragmatic and spiritual intimacy with other-than and more-than human presences, with the spirit(s) of place, with communities that include animals, plants and more. This separation or dissociation of human consciousness enabled the rise of modernity financed by colonial moves the world over. As a result we have the entanglement of modernity/coloniality (Mignolo,

understood and responded to differently depending on its paradigmatic context. Dancing with uncertainty, in its indigenous sense, is the practice of grounded hope based in ceremonial intimacy with inner and outer worlds. Here uncertainty as part of life is acknowledged in ongoing practices of conversations within an ecologically grounded community. Hope and uncertainty are embedded in daily life. By contrast: with the rise of the Western Enlightenment, hope, a word etymologically of comparatively recent origin in the 13th century, moved to transcendental realms and uncertainty

Jürgen W. Kremer, PhD, is the editor of ReVision. His forthcoming book on consciousness is entitled *Native Quantum Cosmovisions.* His other books include textbooks for introductory psychology *(Psychology in Diversity—Diversity in Psychology),* abnormal psychology *(Understanding the Complexities of Psychological Suffering),* and identity and decolonization (with River Jackson-Paton, *Ethnoautobiography—Stories and Practices for Unlearning Whiteness, Decolonization, Uncovering Ethnicities).*

became increasingly framed as the challenge of progress and control, most recently the struggles to control climate change. There is a qualitative difference whether uncertainty is understood within a paradigm of progress and the search for control or, alternately, a paradigm of balancing and nurturing conversations.

Western minds increasingly dedicated themselves to the seeming safety of one-dimensional rationality (Marcuse, 1964) while peoples present to the visionary or imaginal worlds of intimacy with all relations were dismissed as primitive, backward, and in need of enlightenment, i.e., in need of Western civilization. Forests, mountains, rivers, and earth were now ready for extraction to create profits and wealth for the elite minorities in power. This shift is the culmination of a long and complex history with much older multicultural traces. The "received view of science" takes the observer out of the intimacies with our web of life to create representations, a distancing from the world. The normative dissociation of Westernized minds relegated what is intimately woven into Indigenous minds to the world of phantoms. These elu-

a social and symbolic order in which this normative dissociation is seen as natural. We could also say that this is a story of the masculinization of the world, the result of a long history of devaluing, discriminating against and persecuting women, together with other relentless attempts to erase feminine aspects of life. The result of this initially seemingly beneficial move of the Western Enlightenment (in terms of theoretical, pragmatic technological advances) has over time created immense suffering the world over whether in the form of genocides, the destruction of Indigenous cultures, our present climate catastrophe, environmental destruction, unsustainable levels of inequality, or identities unmoored from grounding nurturing conversations, and thus inflamed. The Enlightenment paradigm has maneuvered societies un/ consciously committed to its metaphysics into a dead-end-street, i.e., the intensifying polycrisis of today.

C.G. Jung (1951/1959) didn't mince his words when describing the state of the modern world, its "rationalistic and political psychosis that is the affliction of our day" (p. 84, §140). Delusions are

ded in, from ecology, from ephemeral and visionary spiritual dimensions, from more fluid practices of gender identity, from commitments to community that include more than the human animal. This is a splitting from the intimacy with rivers, mountains, plants, animals, and other beings as relatives, a dissociation from dreams that have the capacity to reach beyond our everyday waking self. Empathy, care, love, understanding, responsibility, mutuality are part of this paradigm that, inevitably, is not conflict free, but in well-functioning communities its participants attend to conflicts through restorative justice practices like ubuntu or ho'oponopono, the spirit of healing and reconciliation.

Here is an example of a contemporary description of such process of relational intimacy and grounded hope by Leanne Betasamosake Simpson (2027, pp. 8 & 23):

Kina Gchi Nishnaabeg-ogamig ("the place where we all live and work together", JWK) is an ecology of intimacy. It is an ecology of relationships in the absence of coercion, hierarchy, or authoritarian power. Kina Gchi Nishnaabeg-ogamig is connectivity based on the sanctity of the land, the love we have for our families, our language, our way of life. It is relationships based on deep reciprocity, respect, noninterference, self-determination, and freedom. (…) This *procedure* or practice of living, theory and practice intertwined, is generated through relations with Michi Saagiig Nishnaabeg land, land that is constructed and defined by our intimate spiritual, emotional, and physical relationship with it. The procedure is our grounded normativity. Living is a creative act, with self-determined making or producing at its core. … Our intelligence system is a series of interconnected and overlapping algorithms—stories, ceremonies, and the land itself are procedures for solving the problems of life.

'Dancing with uncertainty' refers to a practice of living in which relationality is central. The algorithms of the Native natural/cultural world facilitate a sense of grounded hope.

sive appearances on the periphery of consciousness are shunned as fantasies irrelevant to everyday interactions. And so are dreams now largely dismissed as irrational. Plants and animals, whether huckleberry or bear, are no longer relatives to engage with in nurturing conversations and agreements.

While systems emerging from Marxist or socialist traditions are notably different from systems based in the capitalist traditions of Western democracies, both are part of the same story, the story of normative dissociation, the story of separation from visionary and imaginal realms, the story of reductionism or physicalism with its all-pervasive obsessive desire to control and delete uncertainty from everyday life. Both delete stories of nurturing conversations with *all* community members and establish

part of the psychotic spectrum and it was Einstein (1950) who identified the experience of separateness of humans from the universe as "optical delusion of … consciousness" and as cause of our ongoing malaise and lack of peace of mind. My term for the delusion of separateness is normative dissociation, i.e., the disruption of relationality, the splitting from interconnections that are able to naturally feed and ground our sense of identity, that help us face inevitable uncertainties, that generate grounded hope through ceremonial and storied intimacy with inner and outer worlds. Since the Renaissance the European traditions have been in a process of amplifying the power of dissociation by separating from interrelationships, from the relationality of nurturing webs, from intimate conversations with the world the self is embed-

In the European traditions the normal, everyday self of Indigenous provenance became the well-boundaried, closed-off self of Western modernity carrying the self-inflicted trauma of the violation of relationality (Cushman, 1995). The self that was embedded in an intimate process of relating transformed into a dissociative process; it split off from its nurturing connections. Communal relatives now are rejected and you can almost hear "it's for your own good". What was power-with in a web of mutual obligations and nurturance, now became narcissistically focused on the development and increase of personal power and profit, shoe-shining the ego with an empty center and with a voracious appetite for consumerism to fill this gaping hole. This is an addictive paradigm in which extraordinary technological achievements are no longer part of a story of balancing and mutuality.

By contrast, the normal sense of self of Indigenous provenance, by all appearances across traditions, is defined through its processes of relationality. Its ego, its will, its motivation, etc. are osmotically nurtured and contained in a process of intimacy within its local web of life it is a part of, the land lived on. This ego is a humble ego, tempered by humor, playfulness, and ongoing obligations to nurturing relationships. Uncertainty is an inevitable part of these relationships— whether as unpredictability of weather, hunt, and harvest or unpredictability of the results of implementations of decisions—yet, the algorithms of story and ritual offer an ongoing practice maintaining grounded hope in the midst of this uncertainty.

This normal sense of the relational self transmogrified during the process of Western Enlightenment into the individualistic, well-boundaried and masterful self (Cushman, 1995). This is, truly, a disfiguring process. It is a process of self-colonization that is the precondition of modernity/coloniality. This process of self-colonization is reflected in a shift in brain processes from the right hemispheric processes of experience, meaning, and integration as master to the left hemisphere as master, focused on representation and manipulation, the world of discrete objects that can be grasped (MacGilchrist, 2009). Now the web of

life, the cycle of nurturing and being nurtured, is reduced to a world of objects with all aspects of relationality removed. It is this dissociative move, this objectification of our intimate relations that creates phantoms. These imaginal appearances on the fringes of the world of perceived objects have no place in the modern self other than as meaningless fantasies or pathological hallucinations. Now what is normal is defined by the psychology of individualism.

The separateness Einstein identified was not merely a powerful move that enabled the Western traditions of science and technology. The perspective shifted from a concern with staying in caring balance within the web of life to a focus on progress and the control of uncertainty. Significantly, this was a violent move. You might say there was something clever about this self-empowering distancing: what increasingly became seen as a web of distracting and distorting entanglements with different qualities of reality was now rejected, and with it the familiarity and intimacy with the intracacies of relationality that had been part of the cycle of nurturing and being nurtured—thus giving rise to a self-empowering distancing or dissociation. This clever seeming moving was done for the sake of apparent control through the powerful rationalistic explanations of reality. Concomitant we see an increase in emphasis on ego and egoic control. But this process was like banishing a member of the family: you are no longer one of us, you are other, you are a stranger. This banishment was an erasure of practices and memories of relationality. The Real, so to speak, shrank to the real. Reality became diminished.

Ana Teresa Fernández evokes the erasure of 43 students murdered during protest in Mexico City in 2014 in a stunning video in which a woman paints herself black and gradually disappears on screen. *Erasure* (2015) makes the viewer feel what it is like to be obscured

in history, a violent move, for sure. It is an evocation not only of Mexican history erased, but the erasure of Indigenous histories the world over, histories untold in the dominant European discourse, yet remembered by Natives. And it evokes the missing and murdered Indigenous women and girls along the Highway of Tears in British Columbia and elsewhere. And the innumerable Indigenous children killed in residential schools, hidden by the implicit and explicit violence of the dominant discourse.

With the rise of Western Enlightenment we notice the rise of whiteness as consciousness, racist and supremacist in its core. What the Enlightenment covered up are intimate relational connections that now disappear from view, from consciousness. White consciousness becomes identified with a host of issues: civilization, normalcy, (neo)liberal progress, individualism, even emancipation, etc. The creation of whiteness, the rise of normative dissociation, is the creation of phantoms, the violent rejection of familiars in a particular ecology. What was relative, now becomes phantom. The well-boundaried individualistic self is what is considered normal, civilized, and natural.

The violence of normative dissociation is foundational to modernity/coloniality and manifests on different levels. When the tree or the deer or the salmon or the mountain is no longer a relative, then I am freed from responsibility, from mutuality, from intimacy. I can take what I want, I can extract from the land what I want, I can use it to profit, it can be mine. The disruption of relationality gives rise to a particular quality of violence that is distinct from the violence that existed before.

Violence has always been possible and has been present throughout recorded history. The notions of Western civil societies were designed, among other things, to contain unpredictable and irrational violence through its legal

> The disruption of relationality gives rise to a particular quality of violence that is distinct from the violence that existed before.

frameworks (meaning: violence among humans, not violence against other-than-human beings). Humans have always been capable of social violence and local wars, whether as tribal warfare or inner conflicts leading, for example, to the destruction of entire villages considered out of balance (e.g., Lomatuway'ma et al., 1993; Malotki, 2002). This is a quality of violence distinct from the violence of modernity/coloniality.

It is the increasing presence of normative dissociation that arguably enabled genocidal violence aimed at the erasure of whole populations identified as other or primitive. History changed after the

ance of Indigenous cultures may be seen as unfortunate and regrettable (giving rise to romanticism and nostalgia), while presented as inevitable and seemingly natural in the course of progress. At this point in history the white mind continues to destroy what it needs to ensure its own survival and the survival of Earth. In this profound sense genocidal violence, colonial and otherwise, is suicidal. What appears in the other are the phantoms practitioners of the Enlightenment assume they were able to leave behind in their quest to relinquish uncertainty through technological progress. These phantoms have come to haunt Enlight-

resentment as inequality and uncertainty have increased. The increase in a sense of powerlessness and hopelessness is fueled by Western progress addiction that tries to outrun its phantoms. The phantoms created during the rise of the winds of the Western Enlightenment fuel the emotional reservoir of fear and resentment, available to political manipulation. Racism, antisemitism, genocides, poverty, child hunger, etc. are maintained by this reservoir of increasing uncertainty, disorientation, and hopelessness. It is a stockpile of deep feelings, oftentimes unconscious, that is at the disposal for manipulation by the elites of a country. Sjón's (2022) latest novel explores, as he acknowledges in the afterword, how this intense reservoir of intense feelings can be nudged one direction or another, in this case toward Nazism.

disappearance of Indigenous tribes and their languages holding specific ecological knowledge. History changed after the Shoah. History changed after Gaza. Normative dissociation affords an unencumbered sense of rationalistic necessity of the erasure of the other; it facilitates a scale of violence that is immune to feelings of care or empathy. Violence became more commonly impersonal and bureaucratic (Bauman, 2002). Strategies of erasure were and are executed through colonial moves the world over. And they continue to be executed internally, within countries, to erase groups defined as other, whether through forced assimilation, bureaucratic violence, deportation, or incarceration. The world of what Jung calls the 'collective shadow' expanded through external and internal increases in erasure and normative dissociation. With it we find the disappearance of freedom and liberty, their reduction to consumer choices and the click of likes, the self now trained in the habits of entrepreneurial auto-exploitation (Byung-Chul Han, 2017, 2021).

This erasure may simply seem directed at the other, but it is fueled by the haunting phantoms of what the Enlightenment has defined as non-existent or irrelevant, and thus made other. The other gets projected onto peoples who are still engaged in relational intimacy. The disappear-

enment societies as they manifest in a variety of individual, social, and ecological ills. Western self perception is distorted, with phantoms right outside the fortress of the well-boundaried and masterful self (Cushman, 1995), part of the delusion of certainty. The poet Gary Snyder noted in 1970: "the most/Revolutionary consciousness is to be found/Among the most ruthlessly exploited classes:/Animals, trees, water, air, grasses" (published in 1974). He thought that "excess desire, whether for material good or epistemological certainties, was the source of suffering" (Douglas, 2006, p. xiv). The specter of the other looms and the violence against what is other, whether Indigenous or 'other' peoples or the environment, is executed to fortify this boundary and to prevent the disruption of its addictive process.

We may be utterly shocked and disconcerted by the increase in social violence, mass murders, shootings, lone wolf murders (with Anders Breivik as exemplar of someone fueled by the phantoms of the Enlightenment). The rise of what might be called disaster nationalism in an increasing number of countries (Seymour, 2024) is not as mysterious as it may appear at first glance. The pervasive deletion of Indigenous nurturing conversations over the last several hundred years has created a powerful reservoir of

Our fundamental challenge is not a question of progress or technological development or new types of powerful interventions to make a difference in our polycrisis. Any adjustments in the story make a difference, of course. Differences in interpretation of a country's constitution make a difference, of course. Who is elected as president or chancellor or prime minister makes a difference. What the current final word on foundational documents of a society is matters. Who is selected for the supreme court of a country makes a difference. Whether a country has functional unions or not can make a difference. However, all these do not change the foundational story. These are adjustments *within* a paradigm that has been flawed in its beginnings through its originary violence. This originary violence of rejecting relatives and reconfiguring what remains visible as resources ready for profitable extraction remains untouched by these adjustments. The violence at the root of the story, whether in its capitalist or socialist versions, has no space for visionary sovereignty, for the Indigenous intimacy in place that facilitates enacting freedom of a different quality.

Martin Luther King, popularizing the abolitionist Theodore Parker's phrase, inspired the belief that the moral arc bends toward justice. The history of modernity/coloniality with its complex meanderings of gains in liberty and decolonization alongside increases in wealth, comfort, and abject poverty; of seeming increases in equality alongside extreme economic inequality and polarization; of rising dictatorships and fundamentalisms; of neoliberalism, autocracies, and the rise of fascism; of gender equality alongside gender discriminations and persecutions; of advances in health care alongside dismal global rates of infant mortality—these complex, contradictory, and utterly disturbing facts subject Martin Luther King's sentiment to inevitable skepticism and questioning. Given the atrocities of the 20th century and the ongoing rise of fundamentalisms, nationalisms, sectarianisms, and divisive identitarianisms—are we now forced to see the moral arc bending differently?

Until we exit the Enlightenment story and acknowledge the phantoms it has created the hope for justice will continue to fade. For the moral arc actually to bend toward justice we need to exit the current story of normative dissociation, of modernity/coloniality. The moral arc will bend toward justice as soon as we commit to the work of remembrance, the painstaking exploration and presencing of what the original ancestral stories in a specific place mean today. This process of remembrance opens the portal to a renewal which will bring forth what could have been on European lands and the histories it birthed. The moral arc will then bend toward justice in both the colonies and the metropoles.

The winds of delusion that have its origin with the beginnings of the Western Enlightenment, have created a powerful world of phantoms and a reservoir of resentment that may make the dance with uncertainty suicidal, a dance macabre at the expense of millions of people, millions of relatives, and planetary destruction. Yet, the alternate story has always persisted, it has always been there. Transforming the winds of delusion into nurturing conversations with communal and ecological commitments of care and empathy is always possible.

Welcoming the Newcomers—Mistikôsiwak

Stories of first contact outside of the dominant colonial narrative are eye-opening. The following is a description of an encounter with Haudenosaunee

along the Saint Lawrence River during the years 1534 and 1535. Cartier, who arrived in North America "with prejudiced expectations, mercantile and colonial agendas, and no common language", describes how several Indigenous women

advanced freely toward us and rubbed our arms with their hands. Then they joined their hands together and raised them to heaven, exhibiting signs of joy. And so much at ease did they feel in our presence, that at length we bartered with them, hand to hand, for everything they possessed, so that nothing was left to them but their naked bodies, for they offered us everything they owned, which was, all told, of little value. We perceived that they are people who would be easy to convert, who go from place to place maintaining themselves and catching fish in the fishing season for food. (from Phillips & Phillips, 2020, p. 69; originally Biggar, 1924)

Kent Monkman's *Mistikôsiwak (Wooden Boat People)* counters such stereotypical descriptions of Native passivity, lack of shrewdness, and naiveté in his exuberant affirmation of Indigenous values of generosity and compassion. The painting *Welcoming the Newcomers* (the title of one panel of the diptych) is a precise and inclusive evocation of a past and future memory of what has been and what will be. This monumental painting brings the past into the present so that it may become what it might have been. Commissioned for prominent display in the Great Hall of the Metropolitan Museum of Art in New York City, the diptych was shown first in 2019, the 150th year of the Met. Its scale is commensurate with the momentous theme it evokes. One painting is entitled *Welcoming the Newcomers,* the other *Resurgence of the People,* collectively titled *Mistikôsiwak (Wooden Boat People).*

Use QR code to access image

In the painting *Welcoming the Newcomers* we see a group of Native people on a rock outcropping rescuing and welcoming a diversity of shipwrecked people from different continents, cultures, ethnicities, genders, and different strands of life. Prominent is the trickster figure Miss Chief Eagle Testickle in their out-of-time high heels, with a tear running down their cheek; they are reaching out to rescue a slave still in chains. The people in the churned up waters are exhausted and desperate, with a shark circling their capsized boat. The overall sense emanating from the center of the painting is one of welcome, warmth, relaxed sensuality and sexuality, community, and receptivity. The Natives on the rock have a vibrancy that reflects the complexities of life: from a reflective Hayo'wetha on the left; to a newborn; to an open-mouthed woman watching the circling shark with fright; to a warrior getting ready to aim an arrow at the newcomers; to a welcoming embrace between a Native woman and a European settler now safely on the rock; to a diversity of relationships between people. The emotions on the faces of the Natives range from reflectiveness, to fierceness, to sadness, to joy, to pleasure, to shock, to compassion, and more. A stand is taken, a welcome is offered. The emotions on the faces of the new arrivals range from relief to disbelief, to exhaustion, to distrust, to pain, to desperation, amidst the symbols of colonial settlement they carry: a Christian cross, military helmets, the clothing of "civilization", and one woman seems to be chained to her rosary. Animal and plant life are part of the welcoming community on the rock outcropping with a shade giving flowering tree, a crab, and rats (presumably from the capsized boat). One of the new arrivals carries the insignia of a missionary and the history of Indian wars and genocide in the form of an arrow stuck in his side. Different historical layers are interlaced into the painting, from the trickster's high heels to a Native arrow wounding one of the arrivals to the transformation of European art pieces into an Indigenous context of past and future.

The painting represents a pluriversal world as we find different Native cultures on the rock outcropping and newcomers from different cultures and from different continents in the waters arriving on the rock. What is shown as natural here is cultural and gender diversity. What is shown as natural here is the attitude of a warm welcome, of care, concern, vigilance, and compassion. It is a flash of memory, as Monkman brings this encounter of the past into the future of today and beyond. If we understand history as flashes of memory, as Walter Benjamin (1974) does (and, as I would contend, Indigenous peoples do) the creation of *Welcoming the Newcomers* is

live models or specific historical Native people rather than generic, stereotypical images of Natives. The Native warrior as noble savage in the style of the Italian Renaissance depicted in a sculpture by Henry Kirke Brown (*Choosing of the Arrow,* 1849) becomes a fierce warrior seemingly intent on resisting settler invasions. Augustus Saint-Gaudens' *Hiawatha* (1871-72), famously misrepresented in Longfellow's epic poem, is liberated, with accurate tribal insignia, as Hayo'wetha, the co-founder of the Haudenosaunee confederacy. Hermon

material. Viewing this and other Monkman paintings invites us to engage in the work of remembrance of Indigenous presence buried under the linearity of Eurocentric depictions of history. The welcome the new arrivals are given helps us (post)moderns of non-Native mind to recognize it as flash of awakening (see also Barad, 2017). It brings the past into the present so that it may finally become what it might have been, a continent held by caretakers of all genders and cultures in their Indigenous minds. No, not a perfect world, for sure, but a world of a qualitatively different paradigm, and that is what matters.

a flash of memory, an evocation of the entanglement of past and present. What flashes up is as much about the past (and its untold and denied Indigenous histories) as about our Indigenous futures. It points to what might have been. With the creation of this painting the past has remained open to become in the future what it might have been. This timely painting brings "not-yet-conscious knowledge of the past that has the structure of an awakening when retrieved" (Benjamin, 1982, p. 491, fragment K 1, 2 transl. from Benjamin, 1999).

While the history of European painting and sculpture is well-known in the dominant cultural context, Monkman's inversions of historical material housed at the Met awakens not-yet-conscious knowledge of the past into the present, it brings the phantoms of normative dissociation into focus. His inversions are pointed and precise, hence powerful and transformative, as Phillips & Phillips (2020) have shown. What flashes up is an Indigenous future through the remembrance work of European art history. *The Natchez* by Eugène Delacroix (1823-24/1835), marked by grief and despondency, is transformed into an image of joy and pride. *The Mexican Girl Dying* by Thomas Crawford (1846) becomes a sensuous presence with the mortal wound and her inaccurate tribal accoutrements removed. Monkman flashes the past into an Indigenous future by using

Atkins MacNeil's romanticized sculpture of a Lakota initiation ritual (*The Sun Vow,* 1899); *The Crouching Aphrodite of Doedalsas* (Unknown, 1600s-1700s), caught off guard, controlled by male gaze; and Titian's *Venus and Adonis* (1550s) all become Native presences. Gustave Courbet's *The Woman in the Waves* (1868) is now ensnared in her rosary, or so it seems, and the male gaze is ameliorated by her suffering face and her apparent imprisonment in the dynamics of colonial settlement.

These imagistic flashes of memory are grounded in the subversion of the actual European history of art; this way the memory of Indigenous stories is made visible not only as corrective for the past but as memory for the future of what visionary sovereignty, the right to envision one's life freely in a particular place, might mean. The precision of the inversion makes its revelations so much more powerful.

This flash of memory created by Monkman is the work of remembrance and, as Butler (2016) notes, "remembrance works against history, undoes its seamless continuity" (p. 102). Memory is like the capture of an event in a still photo, presumably truthful. By contrast, remembrance is the ongoing work of remembering as we round out the complexities of history, trying to resolve the tensions between the reigning stories and stories relegated to collective shadow

This is the painting's revolutionary potential of reversals and remembrances, its evocations of an alternate stories that have always been there. In these stories dancing with uncertainty meant and means engaging in nurturing conversations, in rituals and ceremonies that aim for balance, and thus nurture grounded hope. It is the remembrance of an Indigenous science and praxis of presence, the remembrance of visionary sovereignty flashing up in the present dangerous moment of careless and violent overwhelming uncertainty.

Monkman's painting does not depict a nostalgic memory to be dissected in academic seminars or to be celebrated in romantic fantasies; instead it awakens as the "red pill" of coming-to presence, the potentially un/settling truths triggered by the red pill as seen in the movie *The Matrix.* Its imagery brings the phantoms of normative dissociation as disturbance into the center of contented ignorance the blue pill induces. Phantoms are welcomed as presences that have always been there, hidden behind the veils of normative dissociation. Instead of framing the painting, somewhat dismissively, as provocation, we need to acknowledge it as a material intervention in the making of time and history. It has interrupted the linearity of the story in which Indigenous mind is a memory of a distant and now useless past.

Similarly, the work (the inquiry, the research, and the ritual practices) of recovery of indigenous mind (for those of us who are out of our Indigenous minds), the work of the remembrance of visionary sovereignty, the engagement with decolonial practices—all of these are material interventions in the making of time and history; they are not merely a process in mind or consciousness, or a mere fantasy or fantastical image. Flashes of remembrance are never merely psychological. The assertion of sovereignty of Indigenous cultures and the recovery of indigenous mind for those disconnected, ritually re/constitutes our mind/matter intra-actions. Consciousness and matter—mind and matter—are intimately entangled (Barad, 2007). It is the work of manifesting the pluriversality of native quantum cosmovisions, everybody's indigenous sovereign capacity to envision and co-create their world. It is the affirmation of Native liberty and visionary sovereignty, the claim to the option of engaging with uncertainty in a process of grounded hope based in Indigenous science and ceremonial work of balancing. No, this is not a rejection of the accomplishments of the Western sciences, instead it is their subsumption on the basis of relationality. The algorithms of stories, ceremony, and place provide the guiding coordinates.

The flashing up of images of indigenous nurturing conversations and their ritual presence, asserts the visionary sovereignty Indigenous peoples have always claimed for themselves: to live in their local ecologies in a balancing process. And the flashing up of images like *Welcoming the Newcomers* gives those of European mind the chance to break the progression of normative dissociation and to fight the history of self-colonization and modernity/coloniality. The trauma of normative dissociation at the root of modernity/coloniality is part of the creation of empty time and linear causality—but remove the dissociation and you remove linear understandings of history and now indigenous constellations flash up and can be remembered. What was phantom now becomes an intimate participant in the intricate balancing network of stories, inquiries, ceremonies, and place. Indigenous presence allows the manifestation of healing and balancing. The past flashes into the present to become what it might have been. Asserting and claiming the stories that have always been there and that continue to be there manifests the grounded hope of decolonial dances with uncertainty.

Feather dancing on the wind
Alighting on the rock of remembrance
Play of obligation

References

Barad (2007) *Meeting the universe halfway.* Duke University Press.

Barad (2017). What flashes up: Theological-political-scientific fragments. In C. Keller & M.-J. Rubenstein (eds.), *Entangled worlds.* Fordham University Press.

Bauman, Z. (2002). *Modernity and the Holocaust.* Cornell University Press.

Benjamin, W. (1974). Über den Begriff der Geschichte (Theses on the philosophz of history), Gesammelte Schriften Band I(2), pp. 691-704. Suhrkamp Verlag. Translation: H. Zohn, (1968), *Illuminations,* Schocken Books.

Benjamin, W. (1982). *Das Passagen-Werk. Gesammelte Schriften Band V.* Suhrkamp Verlag.

Biggar, H. P. (Ed.). (1924). *The voyages of Jacques Cartier.* University of Toronto Press.

Butler, J. (2016). One time traverses another: Benjamin's "Theological-Political Fragment". In: C. Dickinson & S. Symons, *Walter Benjamin and theology.* Fordham University Press.

Cushman, P. (1995). *Constructing the self, constructing America.* Addison Wesley.

Douglas, A. (2006). *Introduction.* In J.Kerouac, *The Dharma bums.* Penguin.

Einstein, A. (1950, Feb. 12). Letter to Dr. Marcus.

Fernández, A. T. (2015). *Erasure.* (Video). Denver Art Museum.

Han, B.-C. (2017). *Psychopolitics.* Verso.

Han, B.-C. (2021). *Capitalism and the death drive.* Polity.

Jung, C. G. (1951/1959). Aion. Princeton University Press.

Lomatuway'ma, M., Lomatuway'ma, L, Nmingha, S., & Malotki, E. (1993). *Hopi ruin legends: Kiqötutuwutsi.* University of Nebraska Press.

Malotki, E. (2002). *Hopi tales of destruction.* Bison.

Marcuse, H. (1964). *One-dimensional man.* Beacon.

McGilchrist, I. (2009). *The master and his emissary.* Yale University Press.

Mignolo, W. D. (1995). *The darker side of the renaissance.* The University of Michigan Press.

Mignolo, W. D. (2011). *The darker side of Western modernity.* Duke University Press.

Mignolo, W. D., & Walsh, C. E. (2018). *On decoloniality.* Duke University Press.

Phillips, R. B., & Phillips, M. S. (2020). *Welcoming the newcomers:* Decolonizing history painting, revisioning history. In: *Revision and resistance* (pp. 68-77). Art Canada Institute.

Seymour, R. (2024). *Disaster nationalism.* Verso.

Simpson, L. B. (2017). *As we have always done.* University of Minnesota Press.

Sjón (2022). *Red milk.* MCD.

Snyder, G. (1974). *Turtle Island.* New Directions.

Facing the Emergent(cy) Future By "Electing" a Different Past

James W. Perkinson

The rain drop fell gently on my hand

And then astonishingly, she spoke

"Help me. I'm dying. Of plastic."

I stopped in my tracks.

Wondered if I should rush to Emergency.

Was I losing my mind?

A raindrop, speaking?

But she interrupted, even more faintly.

"MAGA," she whispered.

"MAGA, MAGA."

"May Adam Give-up the Apple."

It was a prayer. Of a raindrop.

Then the water evaporated. Became air.

Fortunately, and unfortunately,

I hadn't stopped breathing.

Yet.

Dr. Jim Perkinson is a long-time activist and educator from inner city Detroit, where he has a history of involvement in various community development initiatives and low-income housing projects. He holds a PhD in theology from the University of Chicago, with a secondary focus on history of religions, is the author of *White Theology: Outing Supremacy in Modernity* and *Shamanism, Racism, and Hip-Hop Culture: Essays on White Supremacy and Black Subversion,* and has written extensively in both academic and popular journals on questions of race, class and colonialism in connection with religion and urban culture.

Introit

A title. A poetic riddle. An invited commentary. Obviously, we are in an emergency. But how long has it been so? And how broad is the geography?

The invite here was for response to "the election." A word already hosting a trove of ghosts, a layer, multiple layers, of significance. I am learning from indigenous counsel of more than a decade now to pay attention to etymologies, to word-genealogies, to the history that our modern world in all arrogance designates "pre-history," hidden up inside our words, or better, gestating inside their roots. "Election" in the context of the contemporary United States of America, hints a different ramification altogether. Since the late 18th-century we pride ourselves on a supposed "revolution," arcing from English monarchy to "American" democracy. An election of representatives "of the people, by the people, for the people." An election by a supposedly "exceptional" people. "American exceptionalism" there for all to see!

But which people? The original "Americans"? Native people? Turtle Islanders? Where I currently reside at the strait called in French, *détroit,* but in Anishinaabemowin, *waawiyatanong,* "where it (the water) goes around"—the Ojibwe? Or Ottawa? Or Potawatomi? And our current "elected" President hums and smirks and deadpans and pontificates: "Make America Great Again."

"Make America Great Again." But yes, which "America"? What people?

But yes, which "America"? What people? Even within the first 50 days of new policy, it is obvious he does not mean the first Americans. Not the Three Fires groups I just mentioned. Or the Haudenosaunee. Or the Lakota. Or Diné. Etc. Already the preference is clear.

MAGA intends (and pretends) to serve "the elect." A charged term: a self-designation of those who began to show up after 1492, sure they were indeed "the chosen." "Christians"—with a self-adopted mandate "direct from God" to "civilize," "missionize," clear out, clean up, cut down, plow up, dig, mine, plant, and otherwise render productive for elite appetite, all land on the continent (actually, on the earth, but we'll stay focused for the moment on *this* geography, between the Atlantic towards which the sun rises and the Pacific in the direction where it sets).

Democracy in its earliest reference indeed meant "people power," *demos-kratos* in Greek. But only fully "peopled" people; only those considered

to be "real people"! It did not include native-dwelling "questionable people" or melanin-endowed "non-people"— such as those already residing here or those pirated from the Mother Continent ("Africa" in the English tongue) to labor as "tools" on the land taken from those original inhabitants—people who looked, dressed, spoke, danced, dwelt, and worshipped differently from those doing the naming and electing. It did not include female persons even if they "looked right." Or even "right-looking" male persons if they did not have property. A democracy of propertied males for propertied males. Whose light skin tones vis a vis these other bipedal creatures would soon enough be designated "white." Pink when washed, red when embarrassed, yellow when afraid, blue when cold, "white" men. With weapons-in-hand as prosthetic extensions of their apparently too-small organs. Democracy. Election. Can't we go back there?

Such is the riff of a poet who matches some of the favored skin tone in trying to begin to write about the most recent, obscenely expensive, PR absurdity we call "elections." Two-hundred-and-ninety-million Musk dollars to weight the outcome in a particularly "orange" direction—to "get rid of waste and enshrine a policy of efficiency." Five-and-one-half-billion dollars by both presidential candidates together. And $15.9 billion for all races. Money to ensure money controls. But enough riposte for a moment.

Let me analyze in a more modulated tone, before returning to the beginning poem—the real sum of the opinion being sketched here. A few days before

the election, I posted for the first and only time in my life on Facebook. I did so to try to give broad perspective on what I thought was materializing before our eyes. I will largely quote from that articulation in what follows to give summary formulation to what most exercises my concern in this hour. The introit (already offered) "vented" that concern.

The Facebook enumeration sketches its bureaucratic policy "face" and briefly augurs some of its underbelly—a visceral conundrum that actually dates back before the founding of the country itself. And even that depth condition, I will suggest, is the more recent concatenation of a historical conniption 5,000 years in the making, now roiling an entire globe. This latter throbs at the heart of the opening poem and will occupy the larger compass of what we consider below. But first, Facebook:

A Brief Foray

Two weeks ago, I voted for Kamala Harris on a mail-in ballot. But it was not a vote for the Democratic Party, whose refusal to address the genocide in Palestine *as a genocide* had me raging regularly (as well as protesting continually). It was a vote against Donald Trump.

My vote against Trump was not a vote against the man. It was not a vote against a despicable character who is a convicted felon, convicted sexual abuser, fraudster, slum lord, etc.—worthy as that rejection might be. It was a vote against what is behind and underneath him, for which he is a temporary "tool." It was a vote against a *movement.*

That movement is not Trumpsterism.

It is a movement that has been marshaling under the surface of our society for more than fifty years. It does not have a single name. But terrifyingly, it does have a 922-page "playbook of policies" spelled out in detail in Project 2025 and a very clear plan of implementation to put such immediately in place by way of Schedule F.

Schedule F of the plan anticipates rapid re-classification of as many as 50,000 Federal employees into "temporary" job status such that they can be fired with impunity and replaced with a bureaucratic army of "true believers" who will implement the policies. Those policies are comprehensive, devised by dozens of former Trump officials now working under Heritage Foundation sponsorship, championed in a book by one of them, the Foreword for which was written by Vice Presidential candidate JD Vance. Trump and Vance attempts, pre-election, to distance themselves were pure posture, a sleight-of-hand "con" as is now clearly evident.

In effect Project 2025 seeks to "gut," abolish, de-fund, or cripple the following:

- Voting (democracy replaced with theocracy)
- Department of Education (to be replaced by party-controlled propaganda)
- Libraries (defunded and closed)
- Health care (Obamacare either abolished or eviscerated)
- Social Security (vastly cut)

- Medicaid (abolished); Medicare (privatized)
- Unions (made illegal or sued out of existence)
- Protest (met with military response, imprisonment if not killing, maybe concentration camps designed for such)
- Abortion (banned nationally)
- LGBTQAI+ identity (suppressed)
- Press (dismantled or made a mouthpiece for the President through law-

suits, regulations, etc.)
- Department of Justice (weaponized to go after "enemies" political and general)
- Climate action (made illegal)
- AI Regulation (instead, AI mobilized in service of security, surveillance, police control, military assault, reduction of insurance claims, health care claims, etc.)

While these policy goals are already

gathering steam in the Dominionist Theology initiative, finding organizational form in the New Apostolic Reformation (NAR), growing out of the evangelical and charismatic movements of the earlier 20th century, the Shepherding Movement of the 1970s and 80s, and now championing the Seven Mountain Mandate, committed to abolishing "separation of church and state" and "democ-

4. *Billionaire Venture Capitalists and Digital-Tech Corps.* manipulation of political power and social perception (building on the long history of Fossil Fuel Companies and Weapons Manufacturers doing the same) many of whose leading figures (e.g., Elon Musk, Peter Thiel, etc.) are increasingly involving themselves and their blood-soaked "wealth" in these above movements to further their agenda for themselves as articulated in one recent publication:

"He [Musk] and the Silicon Valley MAGA cohort were finished with Democrats, regulators, stability, all of it. They were opting instead for the freewheeling, fortune-generating chaos that they knew from the start-up world. They had big dreams and had made the calculus that Trump would create a more hospitable environment in which to realize them. They were going to plant devices in people's brains, replace national currencies with unregulated digital tokens, replace generals with artificial intelligence systems and much more. 'Technology is the glory of human ambition and achievement, the spearhead of progress and the realization of our potential,' Andreessen wrote in his manifesto. 'We are not victims, we are *conquerors*.'"[1]

The Facebook articulation wrapped up with confession and characterization thusly:

> The pre-November 5 status quo was a festering wound just waiting the right pathogen to metastasize into blistering infection.

deeply alarming, it is the 50-year-old "force field" they now coalesce that is the real emergency. Underneath, all around, and animating Project 2025 are four major *movement* groundswells now converging into a veritable flood. These include:

1. *White supremacist mobilization* embracing the *Turner Diaries* as its "bible," written in the later 1970s as a novelistic vision of white power, moving from a tiny minority on the far-right fringe step-by-step into the political mainstream by way of continuous activity in "cells" until able to emerge as a "Party." The Oklahoma City bombing carried out by Timothy McVeigh in 1995 and the January 6 assault on the capitol in 2021 were "featured organizing events" anticipated in the novel. The Proud Boys were passing out the *Diaries* on the streets in the January 6 event. This white wet dream "maps" emergence into a major party, take-over of the country, and then by way of nuclear war, take-over of the planet for pallid-skinned men. Clearly, we are already at the "Party" stage in the recasting of the Republican Party as it now is. Yes, it is just a novel. But it is functioning for many as a bible.

2. *Christian Nationalist* takeover of institutional and political life and public discourse, beginning with the Moral Majority in the 1970s,

racy," taking over the seven major forums of society (family, religion, education, media, arts, entertainment, and government), recasting them as a pyramidal structure now to be run by Christians alone (primarily men), pushing their agenda as a spiritual war pitting themselves as the sole forces for good, fighting against all opposition as "demonic" and thus not to be reasoned with or negotiated over, but dominated and obliterated.

3. *Militant gun culture*, emerging out of the pre-history and early years of the country requiring every white male to function as surrogate police,

> If there was no soul, there was no human, if no human, then no problem.

on prowl to catch fugitive slave-runaways and to kill remaining Native Americans, historically gaining shape and political cache in the NRA, but now broadly enculturated to the tune of more than 400 million guns in the country, overwhelmingly owned by white males (62% of all gunowners), and a visual culture (TV, social media gaming) that basically posits metallic "arms" as the essential emblem of valid masculinity, a veritable prostheses of that identity.

I do not pretend to be prescient or "crystal ball clairvoyant." I deeply hope I am wrong. But if I was speaking to a Christian audience, I would venture that the above could perhaps be understood as the outline of a convergence of "Principalities and Powers" the like of which the planet has never seen before. Or in another articulation, Project 2025 is the Doctrine of Christian Discovery in full bureaucratic dress and policy detail, coming back up from the underbelly of the country, never having been faced or repudiated in its genocidal disappearance of Native folk, enslavement of African folk, and invasive rapacity plundering sovereign places elsewhere on the planet 553 times since the (Stannard, x, 11). Of course, the exact details, in concrete locations remains the subject of intense dispute—especially given that the "historical records" of such have to be conjured and augured from the texts of the Euro-colonizers

What was now to be "capitalized" would have to be pulled up from the land.

Native folk resisted enslavement as an incipient worker-class by fighting back, fleeing west, or dying of disease. And Euro-colonizers quickly decided what they wanted from indigenous communities was that they "be gone"—that they disappear; their only utility was the land under the feet. But how convert that stolen land—savagely cleared of its indigenous occupants—into wealth transportable back to the European homeland? Menial and criminalized European labor brought over often enough did not survive the climate extremities of this new "American" geography and the answer to the resulting conundrum just as quickly became a concentrated "reach" into "Africa" to purchase human muscle to work land into mineral and crop, to mine and cultivate. And how remake a human being into a productive tool? By theology initially, by "painting" the upright bipedal humanity into a "spirit-vacuity" consisting only of bone and brawn "like cattle."

A concerted theological construction of "black flesh" as devoid of a savable interiority called a "soul" underwrote

country's founding, according to the Congressional Research Council report of 2010.

Obviously that pre-election "belch" of concern is now gaining flesh (and getting rid of such) in an executive-order "flood and fury." And it demands utmost opposition and challenge for the foreseeable future. In every way possible.

Supremacy's Genealogy

But it also demands equally fierce questioning and contextualization. The emergency is not alone this particular country's sudden implosion. The pre-November 5 status quo was a festering wound just waiting the right pathogen to metastasize into blistering infection. The quote above of the 553 incursions on sovereign terrain elsewhere since 1776 is itself omen. The country has been built on violent conscription of peoples and more-than-human creatures ("resources") in service of an ever-more-complexly elaborated Euro-Christian and capitalist agenda at every point along the way.

Certainly, the country started that way. The US began in a program of genocide the depth and extent of which had never been seen before on the face of the planet. With estimates of between 75 and 145 million native peoples, from the top of Canada to the bottom of Argentina, dwelling in varied cultures and communities and lifestyles when Columbus first set foot on dry land (in present day Haiti/Dominican Republic) in 1492, a 95% "disappearance" rate across the Hemisphere over the centuries following represents a tally of terror and brutality that has never elsewhere been matched

themselves, largely committed to legitimizing the devastation as a necessity of the priorities of "civilization" and "Christianization."

And of course, Columbus' venture—as indeed of those who followed—was at core economic. For him—a concern to get to the spices of India and the silks of China by going "backdoor" (he thought) on Islamic control of the Mediterranean basin and points east along the Silk Road. Europe of the day was basically a relatively "backward" domain on

the edge of a sophisticated continuum of Muslim societies and had been since the collapse of the Roman Empire by the 6th century and the advent of international Islam from the 7th century onwards. Portugal's success in trading for Congolese gold in the 15th century, catapulted Spain westward in search of economic leverage capable of competing with this upstart neighbor. And once landing and beginning to get a sense of the extent of what they had "bumped into" and after gathering up (stealing, that is) all of the "loose change" of gold and silver artifacts, discovered in the native communities they subdued and conquered, within a decade or two of their arrival, the new "necessity" was a question of labor.

the entire enterprise of "chattel" slavery (Earl, 5, 16). The initial racialization was by means of spiritual erasure. If there was no soul, there was no human, if no human, then no problem. What was inside a shackle was no different than what was under a yoke. Whether chattel or cattle—the import was a tool for produce and finance and commerce. And that rapidly convened regime of labor to re-engineer stolen land into mobile riches itself occasioned the second largest genocide in human history. Behind each African incarcerated in a slave ship, transported across the Middle Passage waters, and delivered, upright and breathing and exploitable to a Caribbean seasoning island and "American" auction block, lay 3 to 4 dead African bodies, put six feet under in the process of shackling that still moving body (Stannard, 317-318, ftnt 9).

Native genocide tallied as high as 135 million people depending on the calculus of population numbers at point of contact and how "genocide" is construed as an intentional project—each the subject of intense scholarly disputation (not surprisingly given the concerted and continuous Euro-predilection to present colonization as "advancement" and "civilization") (Stannard, x, 11). Under similarly motivated contestation about numbers and scholarly "construction," African genocide registers as high as 50 million (Stannard, 317-318). Even if only the lower end of the calculations is given credence in each case, the actualities of these events remain the most horrific in history—and in regard to Native America, even registering geologically as the Little Ice Age of the 17th century due to so many agricultural communities "disappearing" and so much carbon being re-interred by the re-emergence of forests (Davis and Todd, 2017).

When Grief Is Not Metabolized

With such a relentless projection of PTSD-inducing aggression structuring the nation's earliest psyche—itself complicated by all of the early capitalist, closing-of-the-commons and witch-burning trauma of late medieval Europe—it is not surprising that this people has gone on to violate other sovereign space on average of once every six months (the 553 times reported by the Congressional Research Council of 2010) for the duration of its official life. An indigenous characterization of the history would likely flare with dire concern: "Beware the hungry ghosts!" Beware the unprocessed bile, the biochemical mix of self- and other-loathing, each compounding the other, offering only belligerent rage as feasible posture. A recently viewed exposé of white nationalist and neo-Nazi extremism (*Healing from Hate*) captures the physiognomy: the singular visage of the "taking back their manhood" adherents in street rally and basement party alike, radiates such rage, offering bulging jugular and grimacing teeth as badge and art. But beneath the veneer, one can only surmise uninhabitable lostness and unintelligible confusion. "What is this whiteness that I supposedly am, if not ontological superiority over every other appearance of human skin and culture? Watch me verify it at the point of my gun!" But at the trigger end of that encounter there is little that has been compellingly creative or grandly astonishing. The whiteness so postured is finally evanescent, empty.

But it is also only a late cipher for this insatiable windigo that began to emerge in and *as* modern history, salivating and savage with desire (Kimmerer, 306). Before it was identifiable as whiteness it was Christian and "elect." And certain it owned the earth—everywhere! After all the planet belonged to God and short of that Being's actual physical presence, its soil and water alike devolved to His proxies, whatever prince or potentate claimed certification under that deity's sponsorship, imaged in His own representative emissary and offspring, Jesus. The resulting Doctrine of Christian Discovery, affirming sovereign right to soil everywhere as long as not contested by a similarly disposed power, claiming similar Christic sponsorship, imported papal bull-ying into property lawyering, giving fee simple title solely on the basis of Christian self-certainty and reducing all other human "standing" on the planetary surface to mere occupancy, subject to termination and removal at the pleasure of the Christian "overlord" (Newcomb, 59, 67, 77-78).) Which is to say, white supremacy had a totalitarian father: a Christian supremacy certain of its monopoly on both territory and truth.

All of this is on boil under the electoral outcome just witnessed. And there is much that could and should be said in further outlining its provenience and its projection, but for the remainder here, in a short provocation like this essay, I want to focus yet deeper down and further back. Because the Christian supremacies in evidence (both Protestant and Catholic)—as well as other kindred "world religious supremacies" encompassing Judaism and Islam, Hinduism and yes, even Buddhism's self-emptying eclipse of permanence—are also offspring of an even more rhizomic delusion of superiority, dating back to our earliest city-state elevations of elite ruling classes out of hands-on interaction with both other human denizens of their dwelling place and the entire more-than-human world of creatures with whom they nonetheless remained completely interdependent and co-valent.

The Root of Supremacy

Yes, a book like Graeber and Wengrove's *Dawn of Everything* gives complex witness to ancient developments, allowing as how some early urban experiments may have retained a modicum of egalitarian exchange and communal equilibrium. But it would seem a Rubicon was nonetheless crossed when we began to settle in ever-enlarging enclaves, increasingly focused on surplus production generated by coerced labor, gathered through imposed taxation, articulating a hierarchy of importance and of lifestyle differentiation—those demanding and commandeering the surplus, living "fat" and buffered compared to their enforced labor "supporters," who died early and often by compare (Scott, 2017). Often enough these early city-states—beginning in Mesopotamia and Egypt, but not long after in China and elsewhere—materialized this sense of an ascending pyrami-

particulates now showing face and force in deepest ocean trenches and highest mountains, coming out of taps and weaving through soils, setting up shop in

al encompassment is global, the elite aggrandizement seemingly uncontainable, the resultant extractive uptake and waste-discard intractable. The planet will eventually metabolize the effluent. But perhaps not before eliminating "us."

But which "us" do I envision here? Again, in an essay this short, I can only hint. The record that is estimable is "indigenous." Cultures that seriously embraced their rootage in a given local expression of biodiversity, tailored their collective profile to on-going communion with more-than-human "elders"—plant-life, animal-kin, seasonal-variation, water-cycling, storm-cacophony, wind-visitation, etc.—letting the patterning dictate their cultural rhythm, their language elaboration, their dance enhancement. Many were hunter-gatherer, some horticultural, in grassland or desert, pastoral nomad. None perfectly residing, some also sliding into aggression and destruction, but many learning and abiding. And many alive to the need to embrace limitation, reinforced by ritual proscription and beauty-making as a cross-generational responsibility to ensure ecozone flourishing in on-going reciprocity and gift-economy exchange, anchored in the bioregion (Prechtel, 2005). City-state settlement began our trek away from such a more-than-human valuing until now, in the hands of billionaire techno-imperialists, the agenda is conversion of an entire planet into a machine algorithm likely dominating human imagination and aspiration in an increasingly draconian fashion. Indeed, we are already far down that road with our social media addiction and AI-fascination and submission.

dal scale of value in actual architecture. Urban-centric elevations like Assyrian ziggurats and Babylonian towers gave physical expression to a slowly "enfleshing" sense of species supremacy, a conviction that human concerns and needs outweighed in immediate significance and ultimate import any other considerations of what began to be thought of as lesser species and "beings." And here I am waxing wildly "generalist and caricaturing" of immense complexity and ever-shifting destinies, that I would, nonetheless, suggest began a trajectory that has proven relentless over 5,000 years. And given the shortness of this script, the suggestiveness will have to remain just that. A mere outline that nevertheless has only reverberated with ever-greater clarity and warning in my own reading of things.

There is a line of descendent stretching from those early elites, presiding in palatial estates and temple shrines physically above everyone and everything else and our modern city-states as nodal points of a globalized circulation of natural creatures, ripped from local ecozone interdependence, re-engineered with a vengeance, marketed in glam and glitter, used and abused with scarce a thought for their origins or integrity, until discarded as "garbage," asking water, air, and soil to please evacuate such from the our own physicality if not the planet at large. But the (plastic) chickens have come home to roost. With microplastic

human brains and colonizing digestive tracts across the planet, our "civilizational" ascendancy—our certainty that we reign supreme, enveloped in architecture and armature untouchable by hungry wild teeth or raging promiscuous pest or flowing toxin of waste—is showing its absurdity en masse. The project of elevation into an imagined independence of and mastery over ecology is patently insane. Recycling is not something we do, but something we are. What goes around, indeed comes around—and is doing so.

And across our 200,000-year span of "sapiential" exchange with all else—only those cultures and communities that have most honored that interdependence and mutuality have a track record approaching anything like long-term sustainability. Civilization has nowhere

worked long term (Ryan, 2019). More than 100 such regimes of self-congratulatory supremacy have traversed a now predictable cycle of boom/bust lasting 200-300 years before collapsing in one form or another of "overshoot" apocalypse (Dowd, 2023). Sooner or later, the natural world pronounces "Me too" over the rapine and plunder and weighs in irresistibly. But now the civilization-

And it is this addictive fascination that I think is part condition and part omen. "Possession" by something larger than merely individual identity and desire I take to be constitutive of human "being." Three million years of co-adaptation as hunter-gatherers has outfitted us to be possessed by our respective local ecologies, in rhythmic sensibility, speech cadence, temperature preference, ambulatory pace, gestural grace, and a thousand other indices of a porous boundary between our own somatic physiognomy and our original eco-ambits of nurturance and patterning. We are designed to be as big as a local eco-system. Both

and insane. But I am committed to learning from such wherever encountered in either living community or yet extant mythology and memory. I have dwelt in cities lifelong and on eastside inner city Detroit after eight years of immer-

with Levantine creaturely beings who schooled and nurtured and embodied and revealed what came to be revered as "deity" (Perkinson, 2019). But here I would only underscore one possible take, on one such trace.

Lakota theologian/lawyer Vine Deloria Jr in a short chapter in his book, *For This Land*, sketched out a striking pedagogy of his people's topography, under the title "Reflection and Revelation" (Deloria, 250-260). Under "reflection" he emphasized the build-up of mythic layers of story, attaching to virtually every prominent feature of the home-place landscape as rumination was repeatedly provoked by striking geological formations, seasonal observations, events affecting community members, floral changes, faunal encounters, storm occurrences, etc. Over generations the landscape would have accumulated multiple layers of storied memory such that a mere stroll across the ground was also a traipse through ancestral history. But under "revelation' he noted another kind of experience in which an elder or medicine person stumbled into a particular "place" on those lands—outcrop of rock, grove of trees, canyon recess, etc.—that suddenly "pushed back," communicating as inchoate Subject, reducing human presence to mere object, with time and space standing still, dread prickling the

materially and spiritually. But devoid of such a biodiverse resonance, we fill the gaps with extracted goods and fabricated gods and ingested drugs and mainlined parlance and ideology. Bulging veins and snarling frowns now. A movement possession, that won an election—here, and with increasing virulence, all over the globe, either in the recent past (like Hungary) or the future to come.

And the only remedy I can imagine is to return—at least in vision and schooling and appreciation—to what works. What has worked in three million years of history. Not necessarily as model, but in value and basic orientation. Something kindred to what we now identify as "indigenous" in willingness to recognize and honor genius and wisdom and lesson in our "other-kind" kin. Obviously, the word "indigenous" can be used in multiple overlapping and even divergent references. Here, I primarily intend a lifestyle reference informed by a given land or marine ecosystem over generations, and a human community continuing to recognize the priority of co-evolution with such, entertaining communication and agency coming from these more-than-human relatives and witnesses to requirements of co-creation and mutual flourishing and necessary withering and dying to make room for what, and who, comes next.

The Rain that Weeps

In that light, I conclude with the beginning. I am not indigenous, except way, way back in vague trace and faint hint of Indo-European ancestry before it went urban and Christian and white

sion, began to discover living traces of African and Afro-diaspora conservation of such a memory—in a vibrant though beleaguered culture of percussive celebration and antiphonal intelligence, using call-response energies to survive all kinds of imperialized urban impossibility and coercion (Long, 7, 163, 194-195). Thankfully, I have never recovered from that epiphany, and it continues to course through my own paltry responsiveness now more than 40 years out from the initial revelation. The schooling has been constant and opened me to begin recognition of such traces of a not-yet-obliterated mode of honoring ancestry and ecology still peeking through the

civilizational stomping and disinformation on many sides (Perkinson, 2024 and earlier books).

One of which is inside the very Christian mythology (in the genre sense of that word) whose supremacy I so lament. After decades of re-reading the founding tradition thereof in Hebrew literature and gospel scripture, on hunt for what might have been precursor "indigenous" practices suppressed but not entirely erased therein, I now can scratch the text surface and uncover still pulsing traces of living in relational embrace

hairs on one's neck, accompanied by a distinct sense of "being watched." This place was then understood as surrounded by an invisible limen and verboten, off-limits to the community, a nook or patch reserved unto itself, perhaps guarded and frequented by various animal species (or not), but only ever to be traversed in the future in times of emergency when such an elder might dare enter the sacred space, at risk, asking for medicine or help.

Stepping back from Lakota experience into the ancient Levantine mists of time, what if the Genesis memory of an original "red mud people" (*adam* from *adamah* as collective term), is understood along similar lines? A community living in symbiosis with trees (and perhaps reflecting a trace of an actual such people of the 12th and 11th millennia BCE called the Natufians), having the run of olives and dates and acorns and pomegranates, but at some point finding themselves accosted with a dread sense of limit, reserving one species of tree (perhaps, according to rabbinic lore, the fig) for itself, for wild concourse alone, separate from human affairs. Thus, a Sacral "land communique" establishing a limen at once eco-systemically vital in fact, and pedagogically essential in principle, in reinforcing mutuality and reciprocity—not human priority or supremacy—as the watchword of sustainability and viable dwelling for the generations. What if such an epiphany—the inchoate "unveiling" of a specific threshold of exclusion, a sequestering of some kind of geo-physical mystery—is the beginning of any eco-local "original instruction" for in-dwelling humans, inculcating self-limitation as a mythic and ritual duty of first import?

We then end with our beginning. An election, at a catastrophic threshold, with some of us sitting like a Frodo and Sam on an outcrop of rock, watching lava cascade and wishing for eagles, in which the depth-hope being sounded and re-visited indeed goes back to the origins of the problem. White supremacy, disclosing an even deeper Christian (and world religious) supremacy, itself offspring of the incipient species supremacy that began this trek into apocalypse. How deep is the emergency? How far back the impropriety? Our rain is indeed choking with plasticity. Can we hear the whisper of that wet teardrop? "MAGA. MAGA. MAGA." "May Adam [finally] Give-up the Apple. May Eve give a fig . . . back to a fig." It is impossibly complex. It is impossibly simple. We used to know how to live—and let live—within limits. Do we really think there is some other kind of "solution" that can sidestep such? Yes, "election." From *ex* "out," and *ligere/legere* "to choose." Can we "elect" a living planet—an earth whose creatures live "outside" human chains and demands and disposal? Can we choose ourselves—*within limits*?

Endnotes

[1] Jonathan Mahler, Ryan Mac and Theodore Schleifer, "How Tech Billionaires Became the G.O.P.'s New Donor Class, Elon Musk and a group of Silicon Valley allies have built a shadow campaign to put Donald Trump back in office." New York Times (10/18/2024) (https://www.nytimes.com/2024/10/18/magazine/trump-donors-silicon-valley.html?campaign_id=2&emc=edit_th_20241019&instance_id=137273&nl=today%27s-headlines®i_id=54661955&segment_id=180834&user_id=2a268bc02e89b0f57c05bdbbff3483dc

---

Bibliography

Davis, H., and Todd, Z. (2017). On the Importance of a Date, or Decolonizing the Anthropocene," *ACME: An International Journal for Critical Geographies*, 2017, 16 (4): 761-780, https://acme-journal.org/index.php/acme/article/view/1539

Deloria, V., Jr. (1999). *For This Land: Writings on Religion in America.* New York: Routledge.

Dowd, M. July (2023). "The Real End Times: From Doom to Faith" (PDF), *Progressing Spirit / Progressive Christianity,* https://thegreatstory.org/dowd-the-real-end-times.pdf

Earl, R., Jr. (1993). *Dark Symbols, Obscure Signs: God, Self, and Community in the Slave Mind.* Maryknoll: Orbis Press.

Kimmerer, R. W. (2013). *Braiding Sweetgrass.* Minneapolis: Milkweed Editions.

Long, C. (1986). *Significations: Signs, Symbols, and Images in the Interpretation of Religion.* Philadelphia: Fortress Press.

Newcomb, S. T. (2008). *Pagans in the Promised Land: Decoding the Doctrine of Christian Discovery.* Golden, CO: Fulcrum.

Perkinson, J. W. (2019). *Political Spirituality for a Century of Water Wars: The Angel of the Jordan Meets the Trickster of Detroit.* New York: Palgrave Macmillan Press

Perkinson, J. W. (2024). *Political Spirituality in the Face of Climate Collapse: Of Monsters, Megaliths, Mules, and Muck.* New York: Palgrave Macmillan Press

Prechtel, M. (2001, 2005). *The Disobedience of the Daughter of the Sun: A Mayan Tale of Ecstasy, time, and Finding One's True Form.* Berkley, CA: North Atlantic Books.

Ryan, C. (2019). *Civilized To Death: The Price of Progress.* Avid Reader Press / Simon & Schuster

Scott, J. C. (2017). *Against the Grain: A Deep History of the Earliest States,* Yale University Press, New Haven.

Stannard, D. (1992). (Chapter Five, Endnote 9) *American Holocaust: The Conquest of the New World,* New York: Oxford University Press.

Wi Wanyang Wacipi
Sundance Lessons

Laurelyn Baker

I am not a dancer in the most famil- iar sense of the word. I am an Anishaanabe Sundancer. I am inspired by a ceremonially har- vested cottonwood tree with col- orful bundles of sacred offerings tied to it. I know that the fabric flags of red, yel- low, black, green, white and blue have been affixed with hundreds of sacred prayers before planting the tree in the middle of a lodge pole arbor. I have will- ingly participated on multiple occasions, dancing to the ancient choreography and forgoing food and water for four days. I am happy to follow those leaders who have shown me the true meaning of self- sacrifice on behalf of all living beings. To sundance is to enter into a trance between the worlds. Once I have pledged to dance, you cannot get me to sit it out for anything.

The times I have attended Sundances —either as a supporter or a dancer—in

Laurelyn Baker is an enrolled member of the Little Shell Tribe of Chippewa from Great Falls Montana currently residing in Boulder Colorado. She is a Sundancer and shares the medicine of the Sacred Pipe entrusted to her by her relatives on Turtle Mountain. Her company Visions of Home Multicultural Feng Shui incorporates conscious aesthetics informed by her studies of the I Ching, Tibetan Treasure Vase, Interior Design, and Five Element theory. Her passion to inspire others to see value in drawing on ancestral knowledge guides her in all endeavors which include mentoring, teaching at Ghost Ranch, and writing.

various arbors around Indian Country, have served me well for years. I have danced at the tree for a total of seven years at Turtle Mountain and Rocky Boy Reservations, as well as one held in the Niobrara Grasslands region. In addition, I have been fortunate to dance in the arbor in support of the fasting dancers at Rosebud, Pipestone, Taos, Shiprock, South Park, and Aguilar, Colorado. Once we pledge ourselves to the tree, mysteri- ous forces (be they ancestors or guides) protect us, giving us the necessary forti- tude to endure. This kind of determina- tion extends out into the everyday world in all ways, and in truth, for the rest of our lives. My personal experience has shown me that extraordinary things are possible when done in tandem with spiri- tual helpers.

The great blessing I have experienced in these ceremonial events is some- thing that would not be possible with- out the strength and certainty of count- less prayers reaching their mark. These prayers have been sent out generations into the future, and made by an untold number of traditional people. We are grateful to our ancestors for successfully reversing the Religious Crimes Code of 1883, which forbade Sun Dancing, Ghost Dancing, and many other impor- tant dances and sacred practices. The law was amended in the 1930s to permit cer- tain dances, but not fully rescinded until the American Indian Religious Freedom Act was passed in 1978.

It is hard to imagine what people con- fined to concentration camps (known by their other name "reservations") had to go through in order to avoid the watchful and punishing eyes of reli- gious, governmental and military agents employed to eliminate their traditional ways at any cost. Yet they persevered. They continued drumming and dancing, facing the Sun. The extreme sacrifices of the old ones enabled us to hang on until today. The marrow in my bones still remembers the decimated villages, the forcible abandonment of our native tongue, and the attack on our lifeways, including a dismissal of our deep com- munication with the more-than- human world. Because of the sacrifices of our ancestors, our life is worth living now. Yet these days we have renewed fears of government surveillance. The words "fascism" and "authoritarianism" are now being spoken.

The lessons I seek to bring forward here from Sundance are both practi- cal and spiritual. I will do my best to describe what occurs, although the core essence of what takes place at summer Sundances is beyond words, and some of its more esoteric aspects are forbidden to share.

The physical deprivation of going without our usual comforts of food and water is easy enough to imagine. Being exposed to the blistering hot afternoons that follow the bone chilling predawn lineup is also understandable. The experience of surviving prolonged periods of deprivation under the auspices of a carefully guarded ceremony is great preparation for the emergencies that we frequently hear of in the news these days. I pray that my experience may serve to inspire people to think outside the box when deciding the best method of resistance to wage against the many harmful changes that are happening today.

The Magic of a Sundance

A Sundance is not easy to explain. The tree at the center of the arbor keeps us alive by sending lines of invisible life-giving energy to those tied to its trunk with long prayer filled ropes. This may sound weird and incomprehensible, but

> To Sundance is to enter a trance between the worlds.

I have witnessed this, and other mysterious phenomena like it. Once an iridescent copper dragonfly appeared at high noon to land on a prayer bundle tied to a stick right in front of my constantly moving feet. Another time this same ancient winged one became a vision, bringing me a sip of invisible nectar in a tiny silver bucket to slake my thirst. The days and nights are filled with encounters like this that will never be put into words. But they made me feel blessed and protected.

The Sundance continues to support me long after the dance is over. There have been many times throughout my life when I needed strength, and .unexpectedly, the vision of the Sacred Sundance Tree appears, shining in the full sun. It appears in my visions exactly like it was seen all those years ago, shining through the feathers of my eagle feather fan when I held it up to shade my eyes. I can feel the beat of the drum keeping pace with my heart. I can picture the leaves, ties and flags shimmering along with the shrill eagle bone whistles, and I am reenergized to carry on.

Recently a day of watching too much news caused me to awaken at 3:00 am in a panic. It is during these times when it is especially good to recall the teachings. I can draw upon those nights on the Sundance grounds when a different kind of dance with uncertainty—brought by the Wakinyan Thunder Beings—tested us. This tends to happen at some point, usually after a day or two of stirring the energies. The walls of the tipi light up with a previously unimaginable number of perceived opportunities to be struck by lightning. The constant booming call of their awe inspiring voice is in synch with their strikes indicating a unique type of message from the skies. It is close. We hold firm. We reassure each other that this is just a confirmation of our prayers being heard and that we will be safe. Wakinyan bring a blessing that makes one aware of the supernatural protection of the Medicine People conducting the dance who watch over us as they communicate with Spirit Beings. No matter what disappointing messages the government and media send, I am not worn down with hopelessness; I know there are larger forces at play that will prevail.

My Anishinaabe ancestors were famous for making big life decisions individually and as a tribe based on ceremonial visions and nightly dreams. I dreamed last night that I was in the ocean surfing. I knew I had never learned and felt the rush of panic rise as I looked at the waves. One was coming toward me from the right and another from the left. The dream afforded me enough lucidity to know that this was an unusual wave pattern. I noticed there was a surfboard under my feet, and while I had not yet learned to surf, I knew it was possible for me to learn. I jumped on the board and took a deep breath, bracing myself for the impact, and was pleasantly surprised to see myself navigating the competing currents and managing to stay above the water. Maybe I was not as impressive as a professional surfer, but my first thought upon awakening was that I had managed well enough.

Deep Gratitude

This morning I am grateful the wind in Boulder is calm. Barely a breeze stirs. The quiet outside makes it a bit easier to maintain a sense of equilibrium while keeping a reluctant eye on reports of the cruel, cold and hateful gusts of oligarchic glee blowing out of the nation's capital. The gentle pre-spring day allows me to safely light the pipe and offer smoke from tobacco, willow bark, cedar and sage to the spirits I know are watching from all directions. The Pipe is an integral part of every Sundance. When working with it I feel strongly connected each and every time. That is a good place to make prayers from. Today I am asking for my mind and heart to come together as the fragrant gray swirl leaves my mouth and moves up towards the endless blue home of clouds. Two young cottontails nearby in the grass face off and jump towards each other to bounce paws together in a rabbity high five. "Oh yeah," I say to myself and smile. Migwetch Wabooz. Thank you Rabbit for the reminder. Chi Migwetch, big thanks Spirit for reminding me it is important to use the words of my Ojibwa relatives. I like to say them now and again on behalf of all the boarding school children who were punished if they dared to speak their native tongue, forced into English only speaking or silence. I read that an executive order was just signed demanding English be the official language. So just for fun I'm also going to say Waabigwanii Giziis (Showing Buds Moon) is still going to shine on us in April. The temperature will most likely be unusual in some way, but this year, baashkabigwanii (blossoms) will certainly reach up towards the sun at that time. It is really hard losing our sense of conviction about seasons unfolding in harmony and to then sit with the realization of the never ending implications that come along with that thought. It is also less difficult, but still really hard not to use a special English Only four letter word to describe how I feel about executive orders these days.

When I was a little girl, my family told me everyone was flying the American flag from their porches because it was my birthday. June 14th: Flag Day. I didn't figure that out until I was twelve. In those days my father's relatives ,the Little Shell Tribe of Pembina Chippewa had been fighting the system since the 1860s in order to gain the "Holy Grail" of Federal Recognition. My family lived in a tidy little white house on the edge of Great Falls at the base of Hill 57. They were too ashamed to tell me the people who lived in shacks up there were my aunts, uncles and cousins. I did not discover that until I was in my twenties. After I knew this, my most fervent

flag, but he likes to wrap himself in it in a weirdly erotic way from time to time. His followers have been known to turn the poles that flag flies from into weapons. Let's just say I find it the height of irony that all things Federal are now under attack by Flag Man. It is certainly uncertain what that means for any of us.

Final Thoughts

As I carefully wrap the pipe back up into its antelope leather bundle, the rabbits hop quickly out of my line of sight.

together to achieve the eternal quest for continuing life in a world of uncertainty led to favorable results. With time they observed how interacting in creative ways with different combinations of the beings around them—both the spirits of and the actual plants and animals, stones, fire, and water—gave extra potency to the effects. Moving their bodies in rhythm with cycles of Sun, Moon, Season, Star and Earth in tandem with the More-Than-Human World helped them gain even more proficiency in directing favorable outcomes for health and help in an uncertain environment. Learning to read signs around us to navigate difficult decisions is a skill can help each other reclaim and hone. What old ways will your great great great grandmother send you in a dream? Pay attention to the things she gathers to feed the invisible. Will you have the confidence to recreate in your own way her acts of resonant beauty to share ceremonially with others?

> There have been many times throughout my life when I needed strength, and unexpectedly, the vision of the Sacred Sundance Tree appears, shining in the full sun.

prayers at every Sundance was for the Little Shell tribe to gain status as a valid culture entitled to land and respect. That day did not come for 157 years. But it did come.

January 25, 2020 was the day we celebrated our Federal Recognition. Of course I hopped on a plane and flew to Great Falls. Of course I brought the Pipe bundle I carry. The event took place on the notorious Hill 57 of my childhood--he place I was told I would never be accepted. Long story short, I found myself at the center of the group of men conducting the pipe ceremony. Since I didn't know any better, I asked if I could join and they gave me a seat in the circle. I shared the pipe that had been smoked all seven times I Sundanced. It was surreal to think of the tree and back again to this ceremony. Afterwards at the dinner and speeches many carried photos of their relatives who died without seeing this day come to pass. Hopefully my Grandma Lil was proud of me.

One of the strangest things about the way the bill was finally signed into law making us the 574th official tribe changing our status from Landless to having a land base to claim was the person whose signature made it final. Who was it? I'll give you a hint. That guy shares a birthday with me. I don't know what his parents told him about the American

My thoughts turn to all of my neighbors who work at NIST NOAA that have just been fired here in Boulder. I think of my Little Shell Father who worked his way out of poverty by becoming an air traffic controller. I think of my husband's family who came to visit from Pennsylvania last weekend. His brother has been employed by the Army Corps of Engineers for over 20 years. He tells hair-raising tales of the toxic sites he has been assigned to clean up. One of those places was New Orleans after Katrina. My beautiful, kind and brilliant niece who works for NASA, and her equally gifted sister working in a research department where she is helping to develop off shore wind turbines for alternative energy, both spoke of having to rename the projects they are working on to disguise any hint of climate science. They have to prove their right to exist in their chosen professions to a person who knows nothing about the importance of that work. I think back to the tree as it represents the hopes and dreams of so many. Will we hold firm in the days ahead? Will we be able to forego the usual sustenance and comfort to nurture to the best of our ability all we hold dear?

Humans learned thousands of years ago varying methods for conducting events in the context of ancestral wisdom. They knew that guiding these practices within a community working

To that end I pay close attention to dreams and waking visions. I track synchronicity. Take note of coincidence. Remember I don't believe in coincidence then hop on the trail to see where the omen will lead. When my friend Glenn Aparicio Parry asked me if I would be interested in writing on the topic "Dancing With Uncertainty", I was reminded for some reason of the magnet on my fridge. The words *Things just got super weird—it's my time to shine* are printed above an image of a slightly goofy looking wild eyed bird. The Journal is called *ReVision* he said. I was intrigued. Visions of Home is the name of my business. The plate on my vehicle is VISION9.

The number 9 is a lucky number in my line of Feng Shui work. VISION is there stamped in green and white because I like to drive up to a clients house with the pronouncement that we are most certainly going to create an environment based on our ability to visualize the Spirit of Beauty filling each room. Is the lucky number charm on my car working? The dent in my rear passenger side bumper reminds me that in truth, nothing is ever certain. But I know my car will take me to the next Sundance I am invited to.

A Five-Fold Path of (Re)turning

Weaving the Collective Towards a (Re)turn to Wholeness

Catherine A. Reynolds

This paper was not written solely by me. It was written, in part, by the wind playing through the pile of yellowing maple leaves collecting in the corner of the yard, the fallen apples slowly decaying beneath their tree, the ladybug navigating the edge of my tea bowl, the pearlescent spider web being cast between two branches in the corner of my vision, and the pair of yearling magpies perched on the fence watching my fingers type these words.

With the intention to inspire connection to each of these additional authors, I would like to suggest that the following pages be printed out (double sided, black, and white, and then recycled) and read aloud from the page, outdoors if the weather allows. At the very least, please read one of the stories shared in Appendix A out loud to the land. I see this as a way to honour the aliveness of these words, written not just by me, in a way that reading silently from a screen cannot achieve.

I would also like to suggest the following playlist be played quietly in the background during reading. I believe this will help create a resonance that, when paired with the spoken words (which, in and of themselves, only tell part of the story), will hopefully spotlight a deeper, somatic meaning for the living being doing the reading. https://open.spotify.com/playlist/0lYliZ3XgBU8MYDEl4nPT2?si=7f2e21c2c1a448e7

The Weaving at the Heart of the World

Myths remind us of the importance of knowing where we came from. Sometimes they stand alone, unique to the land from which they sprung. Often though, their elements, storylines, and characters are reflected in one another. These stories belong to all of creation and speak to the universal truths of life. Several, from distinct cultures around the globe, tell of an Old Woman and an animal companion, living in a cave at the edge of the world.

Unaffected by the cycles of time or the seasons, the Old Woman is said to be working on a beautiful weaving. Her tapestry, or blanket, or cloak (this varies from story to story) is in a constant state of being beautifully and intricately made, almost finished, and then dramatically unmade by her companion (who is either a black dog, a raven, or a crow, depending on the culture telling the story). They reside in a hidden cave, along with a giant cauldron filled to the brim with a bubbling soup and the ancient fire over which it sits. Most of the time, the Old Woman is engrossed in her weaving. Every so often though, the soup will utter a splutter and up the old woman gets, moving slowly towards the back of the cave to stir the cauldron. As the Old Woman attends to the soup (which is said to contain all the seeds of all of creation), her animal companion (whose name is Trickster) comes forward. Trickster understands that if the Old Woman's weaving were ever to be completed, the world would come to an end. So, to prevent this, whenever the Old Woman turns her back to stir the cauldron, Trickster takes up a trailing thread from the edge of the loom and tugs. They tug and tug and tug until eventually, the entire weaving comes undone. When the Old Woman returns from the fire, all that remains is a tangled pile of threads beneath her loom. She stands and considers the chaos before her. Some stories say she has a tear in her eye here, lamenting her lost work, but

Catherine (Cat) Reynolds is a Tea Ceremonialist and Nature Mystic. A writer, poet, and a medicine maker, she is happiest out in Nature with her bare feet on the earth and the wind in her hair. Cat holds a master's degree in East-West Psychology and has spent hundreds of hours studying and practicing in a variety of other traditional lineages. Weaving the living philosophies of these ancient traditions into modern psychology, her practice focuses on Somatic Ecopsychology and the Medicine of Nature. Inspiring remembrance of what it means to be a part of (and not separate from) the world, Cat has devoted her life to (re)connecting and (re)enchanting people with the animate Earth.

they notably never mention her lashing out at her companion, or acting in anger of any kind. Slowly, with great care, she reaches down and takes up one of the threads from the tangled pile - maybe that bright green one there – and, with thread in hand, smiling to herself, she begins again.

When Words Were Alive

> Language is a living thing, and the meaning of a given word can change over time. For instance, myth, which in contemporary usage tends to mean something that is false or untrue, originally meant something that was deeply true, something that carried universal truth, and could be as if a living source of emergent truth. (Meade, 2024)

This dance of uncertainty happening between the Old Woman and Trickster creates the opportunity for new patterns and truths to emerge, and for life to continue. The weaving itself (representative of the state of the world, of humanity, and the collective consciousness) in its constant state of being made, unmade, and made new again, reflects a univer-

aloud to remind humanity where we Earth, and to point out the dangers of forgetting this connection. Storytellers would cast the words as spells, taking listeners on a journey, allowing for them to encapsulate themselves into the spirit of the story and the land. The words themselves would change and shift with every telling, as the weaving does with every re-making, bringing forth the truth and wisdom of the specific moment in which they were being shared. So much was held in the old languages. Through the resonance of a human voice, in an exchange with both other humans and the natural world, a certain alchemy of integration and relationship with the animate Earth would occur. We (humans) would become entangled with and enchanted by the places in which we were living, breathing and telling the stories.

Dropped Threads: Humanity's Forgetting

Stories like these are no longer shared around campfires, at hearths, or along the road with fellow travelers. Humanity no longer sees itself as part of nature, no longer remembers what it was to be *of* the land and not simply *on* it. Collec-

nine. The Feminine, represented here in the Old Woman responsible for weaving the consciousness of the world into constant, shifting existence, has been nearly completely forgotten. It is not inconsequential that these structures have enabled humanity to spend the last several centuries devastating our living Earth. As a result, we now find ourselves in a time of deepest discontent, disease, and disconnection.

David Abram (1996) speaks to the origins of the root of this disconnection in *The Spell of the Sensuous*. "All of the early writing systems of our species remain tied to the mysteries of a more-than-human world" (p.96) They were place-specific; consider the differences between the petroglyphs of pre-Columbian Turtle Island and a pictographic system like Egyptian hieroglyphics. However, as language and writing evolved, the way in which we communicated with one another requisitely became more and more generalized. While this generalization and standardization of certain languages and written letterforms doubtlessly made it more convenient to communicate with one another, it inherently cut out communication with Nature, the Earth and the Other. Once humanity began to "noun" those more-than-human Others, every being that would once have been commonly recognized as alive - possessing spirit and having consciousness – was seen dumb, deaf, and mute. The living world around us was no longer full of wonder and magic, it existed solely for the benefit of humankind – ourselves now distinctly separated from and not a part of nature – to use as we wished, without apparent consequence or guilt. For centuries, as the briefest of glances at any current new reels will show, we have done just that.

Humanity as a whole is now standing before the chaos of that tangled pile of threads. We must choose wisely where to begin, understanding that every choice will entail learning some of the steps to the dance of uncertainty. I believe we are being collectively called to remember the languages our tongues and bodies and hearts once knew, begin asked to speak and sing and share them aloud with the Earth once more. To overcome these *mental* structures that surround and

> Collectively, we have forgotten the old stories and the power that comes from sharing them aloud on the land from which they grew. We have forgotten what it means to be enchanted by and entangled with the world in which we live.

sal truth of its own. Uncertainty is an inevitable part of life, but like the Old Woman, we get to choose how we face it.

Stories like this[1,] along with an infinite number of others, were once known to be alive with truth and wisdom. They were the guiding threads through the labyrinth of life, the pathways on which humanity was able to locate itself within the greater tapestry of the world, not above but right alongside every other being we share this planet with. These stories would be spoken (or often sung) came from, of our deep-rooted ties to the

tively, we have forgotten the old stories and the power that comes from sharing them aloud on the land from which they grew. We have forgotten what it means to be enchanted by and entangled with the world in which we live.

In his book *The Ever-present Origin*, Jean Gebser (1985/1949) highlights how "the mental structure [of our current society now] emphasizes only the one bright, right, conscious, masculine, active side just as it accentuates one god, one soul, and the individual human being..."(p. 198) just as it de-emphasizes the dark, shadowy, unconscious, femi-

beguile us, we must (re)member and (re)turn[2] to where our *bodies* came from. Turning and re-turning along the spiraling paths of the labyrinth of life, we must find and take up a *new* thread and weave a *new* path, in doing so, becoming active members of this animate Earth once again.

The Five Spheres of Consciousness

An Initiation of (Re)membering

Linda Hogan, (1995) asks "how do we learn to trust ourselves enough to hear the chanting of the Earth? To know what's alive or absent around us...the old, slow pulse of things..." (p 28). We must become, as Gebser (1985/1949) described, initiated into the lucidity of Origin. Here, Origin serves as another word for Source, Spirit, God or The Mystery. To Gebser, Origin was the essential thread running through each structure (or layer) of consciousness, the thread that tied All together as One. I believe following this thread requires a certain level of trust, and an honest desire to for us to truly feel "the old, slow pulse of things," once more. We must want to return once again to a place where humans and Origin, humans and Earth, are entangled as a whole. Integration of each of the previous structures of consciousness is required for this kind of (re)turning. To Gebser, integration of this kind would bring humanity, once again, to a place where our relationship with Origin (Earth, Source, Mystery) was one of numinous enchantment.

To attempt this kind of integration, we first need to reach back along the thread humanity has been following for so long, to understand the structures of consciousness that the collective has experienced thus far. My primary aim with this paper is to lay out a path of (re)turning, (re)membering and (re)enchantment. I will therefore cover only the basic characteristics of each of Gebser's structures, as a foundation for understanding the proposed path. As the Integral is represented best by a sphere, I will refer to each structure of consciousness as a sphere moving forward, to honour our aiming for that ultimate wholeness.

The First Sphere: The Archaic

Gebser (1985/1949), defines the Archaic as being essentially identical to Origin; "it is a 'first' structure emanating from that perfect identity existing 'before' (or behind) all oneness or unity which it initially might have represented." During this time in our history, the human soul is seen as being dormant or asleep, and no differentiation exists between people and nature (p. 43).

Not much is known about this ancient time, since language and writing did not yet exist, at least not as we know them today. As such, any written accounts of the human experience during that time would be pale reflections, cast out from a mirror aimed at the past, held from a place within one of the subsequent spheres. Indeed, Gebser himself found only two sources he considered to be acceptable reflections of the Archaic sphere, themselves both written during the Mythic sphere. Zhuangzi's (2009) statement that "the Genuine Human Beings of old slept without dreaming and woke without worries" (Ch. 6 line 6:6) was one of them. In particular, the expression of sleeping without dreaming suggested to Gebser (1985/1949), that consciousness had not yet awoken in or been attained by these early humans, who were still "unquestionably part of the whole" (pp. 44-45).

The Second Sphere: The Magic

The [humans] of the magic structure [had] been released from [their] harmony or identity with the whole. With that a first process of consciousness began..." (Gebser, 1985/1949, p. 46)

With the beginning of the arising of consciousness, human beings started to see themselves not solely as the world, but as part of the world. While a single part (a single human, for example) could still represent the entire whole, we were not completely separate from the world, but existed as distinct individuals within it. Gebser (1985/1949) suggests that, during this Magic structure, consciousness was not quite residing within humans yet but resting, or sleeping, within the Earth herself. Gradually this earthly consciousness would begin to stream towards and into humankind, leading to an emergent awareness of nature as the "recognized" world, while humanity remained egoless. There was an attitude of vital agency, driven by instinct and emotion, alongside a non-

> Stories…were once known to be alive with truth and wisdom. They were the guiding threads through the labyrinth of life, the pathways on which humanity was able to locate itself within the greater tapestry of the world, not above but right alongside every other being we share this planet with.

directional interweaving and acceptance of the unity of all things. Liner time, as we know it today, was non-existent. Nature was humanity's objective external focus, and emotion was our subjective internal focus. (pp. 617 – 621)

The Third Sphere: The Mythical

Where in the Magical sphere, humankind's awareness of self was mainly one-dimensional, in the Mythical sphere, we moved into two-dimensionality and polarity. To Gebser (1985/1949), this suggested an emergent awareness of Soul or Psyche as the objective aspect of the external world, and imagination as the subjective aspect of the internal world. Humanity began to internally reflect and contemplate both ourselves and the world around us and then externally represented these processes through utterance, expression, and the creation and sharing of myth. Imagination arose during this sphere as well, as we expressed our experiences in new ways. Nature still equated to relation, although the focus was more on ancestors (past-focused) than kith and kin (present-focused), as it had been in the Magic sphere. Relationships were generally still egoless., and Soul was still seen as interchangeable with Life and Death, (pp. 617 – 621)

The Fourth (and Present) Sphere: The Mental / Rational

"We can no longer hear the voice of the rivers, the mountains, or the sea. The trees and meadows are no longer intimate modes of spirit presence. The world about us has become an 'it' rather than a 'thou'" (Berry, 1999, p. 17).

This is the sphere of consciousness in which we currently reside. And, as Thomas Berry points out, people are no longer able to hear the voices of Nature, which therefore no longer holds spirit, meaning or importance to our disconnected, rational minds. "The word 'rational' originally comes from 'ratio,' referring to harmony and proportion between things" (Bohm, 1980, p.26). This original meaning is the one to which we must return. The current Western paradigm of rationality generally excludes any experience that cannot be satisfactorily explained by the high and holy trinity of the scientific method, modern academia and the thinking mind.

According to Gebser (1985/1949), the essence of this sphere is duality. Society is externally objectively focused on the concept of space, and internally subjectively focused on abstraction. We relate to the outer world as an entity wholly separate and apart from ourselves. The collective attitude is highly cerebral, focused on conceptualizing, projecting, seeing, measuring, and believing. Relationships are future-oriented and often goal or purpose driven. Where, in previous spheres, relationships were in part tied to our more-than-human kin and the natural world, they are now almost entirely egocentric and materialistic (pp. 617 – 621). By considering each of the spheres that existed "before" now, (another defining characteristic of the Mental sphere is linear time) we can understand where and how humanity dropped the throughline, or thread of Origin. The question then becomes; how do we pick it up and begin anew?

A Merging of the Spheres: The Integral

Gebser (1985/1949), believed that the Integral sphere enveloped and included each and every sphere occurring before it. As the spheres mutated and changed, they did not negate any aspects of their previous iterations, but instead integrated them, merging All together as One. This Integral sphere is the ultimate merging, where the consciousness (of all beings) would be collectively recognized, open and free flowing without divisions or limitations. Humans would be free of the constraints of ego, existing instead in an amaterial, enchanted entanglement with Origin, Soul, and Source. We would step out of the bounding boxes of "time" and "space" and reside instead in an aperspectival, four-dimensional cosmic relationship with the numinous. In merging the spheres and moving into the Integral, humankind would at last be returned to Origin (pp. 617 – 621).

A Pathway of Return

"The pathway of Return begins when the masculine journey away from origin has run its course... The Return leads back to Oneness, wholeness, and healing" (Parry, 2015, p. 160).

Glenn Parry (2015) writes in *Original Thinking,* that humanity needs to deeply examine and question our conditioning, in order to have any hope of escaping our current path of shortsightedness. The path we have been walking centers around seeking short-term benefits only for ourselves, while endangering the entire community of the Earth in the long run (p. 161).

We seem to have forgotten that community includes humanity as well. To scaffold the collective into the Integral, we need pathways that are as multifaceted as nature is. These paths must be integral, accessible, and based on principles of oneness, wholeness, healing and connection. This means they will also naturally include elements (threads) from each of the previous spheres of consciousness, along with the additional thread of Origin that was ever-present (whether pervasive or hidden) within each of them.

A Five-Fold Path

Only by walking and working in the liminal space *between* the spheres (not residing in one alone) will we be able to untangle the tangled, draw up original threads from each sphere that link All together as One and begin weaving once more. The five-fold path laid out below could serve as the warp and weft of humanity's new weaving. It consists of Practices, Partners, Plants, Place, and Pith.

There are three primary strands to this woven path - Partners, Plants and Place. As with all weavings, these primary threads are woven onto two foundational threads, called the warp and the weft. These foundational threads are Practice and Pith. I will describe Practice fist, as one half of the foundation. I will then bring in each of the three primary strands, offering practices and ideas on how to foster a return to right-relationship with Partners, Plants and Place. I will close with an exploration of Pith, the other half of the foundation, diving into the language of Spirit and the expression of Soul. The following practices are only suggestions of accessible starting points; many more exist beyond what I have space to share here. They are opportunities for re-enchantment and re-entanglement; choices of threads with which humanity could begin to re-weave our collective future.

Practices: A Foundation

Practice is the foundation for all other foundations, the warp thread, the base of the weaving. It lays down the bones, the structure for each of the other threads to be built up on. I chose to use the word practice for its neutrality and accessibility, but this thread could just as easily be called Ritual. Each of the practices proposed herin will be more potent, more profound, when pursued with the deep devotion and intention often found in ritual spaces and rites. Any practice, approached with attention and intention, can become a ritual. In our current sphere of mental-centric-consciousness, the cultivation of attention and ritual have been set aside, since they generally require an awareness of and attunement to our own animal bodies. The word Ritual itself holds a fair amount of religious and spiritual connotation as well, which could be both positive or negative depending on a persons' context. Understanding that such perceived connotations and levels of awareness might prevent people from engaging at all, in the spirit of Trickster, we will call this thread Practice instead.

One practice I have returned to repeatedly while walking this five-fold path myself, one that I can say from experience will strengthen and compliment all others, is an apprenticeship to silence.

> You must learn one thing. / The world was made to be free in. / Give up all the other / worlds / except the one to which you belong. / Sometimes it takes darkness and the sweet / confinement of your aloneness / to learn / anything or anyone / that does not bring you / alive / is too small for you. (Whyte, 1997)

In today's world we are more often surrounded by noise than by silence. That sweet confinement of aloneness that Whyte speaks of is a rare jewel, buried under layers of flashing lights, over-saturated colours, blaring sound and rapid movements constantly streaming at, around and through us. Finding time for true silence is almost impossible. So, we must make space for it, both in smaller doses as a daily practice and in longer stretches, as a deeper form of Medicine.

For those daily, smaller doses, five minutes of intentional silence before the day starts (with a focus on doing nothing but being present to the silence), can create powerful shifts in how we interact with the world. Putting down our screens, turning off our phones, and giving our brains space away from the cacophony that technology emits, is also excellent, especially if done for longer periods of time. Acknowledging that unplugging is sometimes easier said than done, this is where longer stretches of more consciously held space can be helpful in solidifying silence as a practice.

> Silence is essential... it transports our awareness beyond thought into a state of what Joseph Campbell, borrowing an idea from James Joyce, called aesthetic arrest. In aesthetic arrest the racing of the mind and heart are stilled, such that we are enabled to feel a sense of our kinship with Being itself, beyond words or concepts or thought. But

we need silence in order to hear that greater Silence. (Smith, 2020)

Silent retreats allow for our focus to be held internally, fostering a renewed sense of kinship with Being. While there is, of course, immense value in community and connection, longer periods of silence offer us a rare opportunity to give those areas of our brain that handle speech time to rest. This allows us to then use that energy for genuine self-reflection, and to remember and return to that kinship. It is important to note that for most people, this is not easy, or comfortable. I recommend first stepping into that sweet aloneness in a safely held container with practitioners who have experience guiding people through whatever will inevitably arise.

"The adventure of the universe depends upon our capacity to listen." (Berry, Swimme, 1992, p. 44). In many different traditions, retreat was a time to work on the primary relationship we have with Self, Soul, and the Land, and to deeply listen to the messages from each. Deep listening sprouts forth from Silence and will enhance our capacity to engage with each of the other practices on the three primary strands of this path.

Partners: Human and the More-Than-Human Beings

If my consciousness has a body, why should other bodies not 'have' consciousnesses? (Merleau-Ponty 2013/1945, p. 408-409)

Partners, the first primary strand of this five-fold path, encompasses relationships and practices revolving around all those 'other bodies that have consciousness,' as Merleau-Ponty expressed (save Plants, which hold a strand of their own that we will come to next.) Partners then, in this context, include both our human and our more-than-human kin here on Earth. I define our more-than-human-kin as encompassing animals, spirits, energies, those who have moved on and any other beings present on the land – seen and unseen. There is deep wisdom and knowledge of the Earth to be gained from observing and working with our more-than-human kin, as all Indigenous communities will attest to. Knowledge that deepens even further with patience and commitment to the work of (re) membering human consciousness into

the animate world.

I have included a simple practice below as a starting point to this (re)membering ourselves back into right relationship with that of all those "other bodies."

An Expressive Art Practice to Engage with Partners

> Inner forms of communication are perhaps the strongest core of ourselves. We have feelings that can't be spoken. That very speechlessness results in poems that try to articulate what can't be said directly, in paintings that bypass the intellectual boundaries of our daily vision, and in music that goes straight to the body. And there is even more a deep moving underground language in us. Its currents pass between us and the rest of nature. (Hogan, 1995, p. 57)

Go to a place in Nature, ideally where it is possible to observe the local flora and fauna. Remember that squirrels, birds, trees and insects have a consciousness that is different from your own, so be open and get curious. Bring a journal and a pen and immerse yourself in this place. Try to set aside your thinking mind and open all of your bodily senses to the experience. Become silent and focused but also allow whatever might be present around you to unfold – sit for at least 15 minutes. Your only task is to witness the Partners that are moving about around you. Introduce yourself to whichever Partners draw your attention; ask (out loud or silently) if any one of them would be willing to sit with you and share in an experience.

Accept a Partner to focus your open attention on. It might be a bird or a body of water, or the wind rustling in the leaves or perhaps an unseen guide that presents themselves upon your arrival and introduction. Whoever you choose to focus your attention on, let them come fully to life in your awareness. Engage all of your senses. Then, slowly and gently, let their energy and their consciousness come into your human body. Become this being as fully as you can, through your body's movements, feelings or voice; feel what it might be like to soar or ripple or gust or pass through time as another. Let this experience be exactly as it is – try not to let your thinking mind take over and categorize, define or ridicule any part of it. If you find your mind creeping in, ask it politely but firmly to sit to the side while you have this experience together.

When the experience feels complete, turn to your journal and write a poem or a few sentences born from this experience, again without thinking too much about it, just let the words flow. Then, as an act of gratitude, speak your written piece aloud with the Partner you just engaged with, offering thanks for the opportunity to re-entangle your consciousness with theirs. Do not forget to let yourself be enchanted by this experience.

Plants: Medicine for Enhancing Perception

The second primary stand of this five-fold path is Plants. For millennia, traditional Indigenous peoples around the world have looked to the plant kingdom, not solely for food and shelter, but also for wisdom, guidance, and Medicine. Entheogenic plants used in religious, spiritual, or ceremonial contexts, often produce a psychoactive or hallucinogenic response in participants. There are a number of sacred medicinal plants used in ceremonies around the world

can help enhance our perception of our human place in the world. As I have my own meaningful relationship with one of these plants – Tea - she is the Plant I will focus on here.

Linda Hogan's (1995) perspective on Ceremony is reflective of my own approach to working with Tea;

> The intention of a ceremony is to put a person back together by restructuring the human mind. This reorganization is accomplished by a kind of inner map, a geography of the human spirit and the rest of the world... Within ourselves, we bring together the fragments of our lives in a sacred act of renewal, and we reestablish our connections with others. The ceremony is a point of return.... But it is not a finished thing. The real ceremony begins where the formal one ends, when we take up a new way, our minds and hearts filled with the vision of earth that holds us within it in compassionate relationship to and with our world. (pp. 40-41).

While not traditionally considered an entheogen, Tea offers a deeply sacred, deeply feminine Medicine. The experience of Tea Ceremony often leaves

evening, Shennong, the Divine Farmer found that a leaf from the tree under which he sat had landed in his cauldron of boiling water. Never one to question the wisdom of Nature, the Sage (who is still honoured today for his tasting and describing the medicinal uses of thousands of plants) bowed to the tree and poured himself a bowl. As he sat drinking bowl after bowl of the amber liquor that steeped out of the leaf, he found the spirit of the tree began to present herself to him. She spoke, in the way that trees do, and told him that she too had been meditating on this mountain, but for millennia. She asked him to tell her stories of the current world, and upon hearing that people now lived in villages and towns below the mountain, requested she be brought to them. She wanted to know what it meant to be a part of human life, to become entangled with it. His spirit uplifted and his eyes brightened by her medicine, he agreed, proclaiming the legendary words that are carved in the rock and brushed to paper, even today. "This is the empress of all medicinal herbs."

In her asking to be entangled with the human world, Tea was offering herself as a connecting thread between humans and Nature. Tea provides a pathway to remembering our inborn relationship with the natural world, offering a gentle way to begin to restructure our human minds and help us remember that we are all part of one great and mysterious Whole. Through Tea our hearts are opened, our eyes become brighter, and we are returned, bowl after bowl, to our Origin within the Integral. Tea reminds us that the seemingly individual threads of the human, the animal, the natural, and the celestial are one; each thing intertwines and is interchangeable. In other words, we can experience the entire universe in every single bowl of Tea. Through my almost nine years of experience sitting with and serving Tea, I can confidently say that She is, in fact, an entheogen.

Tea speaks to us, not in the language of the mind, or ego, but in the language of Nature. Following a Ceremony, there

> Following a Ceremony, there are often no words to describe the experience. What pours forth is nothing short of the utterances of the leaf, the Mystery of the life in which we are all entangled.

with which one could form a relationship. Any quick web search will elicit multiple opportunities to "experience the sacred" or "learn the secret of life," often in just one short weekend and for several thousand dollars. These are not the relationships I am speaking about; we could argue that experiences like these aren't founded on relationships at all, except perhaps with money. That people are monetizing plant medicine though, that the collective is searching for them more and more does speak to their potency and power though. There is no doubt that Plants, when used in ceremony and within a deep relationship,

participants with an expanded perception of their own consciousness as it relates to the consciousness of all beings. Tea provides a map for the ultimate return, as Hogan shares. To illustrate Tea's capacity for this, I will share the legend of Shennong, a mythological emperor in Chinese folk religion, and his fabled first interaction with Tea. With the intention of honouring that old stories are living things themselves, I have chosen to paraphrase this legend in the way I personally share it after serving Tea. One of the many different recorded versions of this story can be found in Appendix B.

Meditating on a mountain one

are often no words to describe the experience. What pours forth is nothing short of the utterances of the leaf, the Mystery of the life in which we are all entangled. It is not something I can write about; it must be experienced.

Place: Entanglement with the Animate Earth

The breathing, sensing body draws its sustenance and its very substance from the soils, plants, and elements that sur round it; it continually contributes itself, in turn, to the air, to the composting earth, to the nourishment of insects and oak trees and squirrels, ceaselessly spreading out of itself as well as breathing the world into itself, so that it is very difficult to discern, at any moment, precisely where this living body begins and where it ends. (Abram, 1996, pp. 46-47)

Place, the final primary strand on this five-fold path, is the one that determines which Partners and Plants will naturally be present and those that will not. Place also defines which Practices will be the most meaningful, and those that might fall flat. Integral to fully engaging each of the threads on the path is forming a deep relationship with Place, as it is through this relationship that all others will root, rise and grow. Any Plant, Partner or Practice can be a doorway through which to access Place, but the most direct is simply to sit.

The Sit Spot

A sit spot is the fastest and most direct way to engage with Place, no matter where you find yourself. The procedure is this: like the artistic expression practice shared above, spend some time, each day, sitting in a spot out in nature, with the sole intention of being present to is. Ideally this would happen out on the land and away from the distractions of home, work and life, but even a backyard sit spot can offer the opportunity for connection when approached with intention. Place underlies houses and roads just as much as it does forests and meadows, although it might be harder to feel. The ultimate location is not as important as the consistency with which you seek to build the relationship.

Once there, the task is to allow your awareness to ebb and flow into the energy of the Place itself. Allow your focus and attention to drift between and around other beings, plants, animals, elements, and weather. Notice what comes up. Cultivate your awareness: notice if any messages, sensations, feelings, or thoughts arrive. Cultivate discernment; where or who are these messages coming from? Bring a journal and keep track of each experience. Go as often as you can, to the same spot, for as long as you can, and notice how the Place changes through different seasons, weather, and times of day.

We must renew our acquaintance with the sensuous world... Without the oxygenating breath of the forests, without the clutch of gravity and the tumbled magic of river rapids, we have no distance from our technologies, no way of assessing their limitations, no way to keep ourselves from turning into them. We need to know the textures, the rhythms, and tastes of the bodily world... Direct sensuous reality, in all its more than-human mystery, remains the sole solid touchstone for an experimental world... only in regular contact with the tangible ground and sky can we learn how to orient and to navigate in the multiple dimensions that now claim us. (Abram, 1996, p. ix-x)

Regular contact, over time, with patience and mindful attention, creates a relationship that, as Abram describes, teaches us how to orient and navigate the multitude of dimensions scrambling and screaming for our attention. Returning to the animate Earth, returning home to that "direct, sensuous reality" is what the final strand of this five-fold path is all about.

Pith: The Animating Inner

Most traditional cultures imagine some sort of soulful presence that accompanies a person throughout the course of their life. But as the narrow sense of rationality and logic has come to dominate modern life, most modern people doubt there is any such thing as a self-defining human soul. And yet, one of the few things that can stand against the onslaught of radical change and great uncertainty in the world is the sense of an animating inner soul... (Meade, 2024)

Michael Meade's (2024) reference to Soul as "an animating inner" essences within each person, is the way I look at Pith. It is the weft thread. Together with the warp thread of Practices, Pith holds the pattern of the weaving, animating and enlivening all that is woven onto it. Pith is ever present; accessible from any place, at any time, by any being. I believe it can be tapped into through each of the practices outlined above and can be interacted with deeply by attuning to its native language, Intuition.

When asked about how the expansion of rationality is different from the expansion of intuition Thomas Berry replied:

With rationality we are never completely satisfied. Expansion of rationality is different from the expansion of intuition, which can bring a depth of understanding and a sense of the sacred... Intuition is the unique quality of the human that is also the consciousness of the earth and the eventuality of the universe because it can reflect on the reality of the universe, its origin and its history. You might say that intuition is the foundation of reason that is laid down first in a child before the rational faculties are added on like grace notes. (Toben, 2023)

> Regular contact, over time, with patience and mindful attention, creates a relationship that, as Abram describes, teaches us how to orient and navigate the multitude of dimensions scrambling and screaming for our attention.

Recognizing that the expansion of intuition often brings a depth of understanding, a sense of Soul and the Sacred, it follows that fostering that expansion could then lead to more meaningful connections being formed. These connections, in turn, would encourage people to perceive and experience the sacred in the everyday, ultimately returning to Origin through those same acts. This is Radical Immanence, this is Pith – where the Divine, the Sacred, the Mystery is not elsewhere, but right here, right now, and available to all of us in every and any moment.

The animating language of intuition, alongside the somatically felt senses that relay intuitive knowing to our brains, only exists *beyond* rationality. We can't simply *know* or *believe* the Sacred to be everywhere, we have to *feel* it in our bones. When a person engages in re-enchanting and re-entangling themselves with the natural world, there will inherently be experiences within those engagements that cannot be organized or specified but that will simply (and deeply) be *felt*. This is Pith – the heartwood of our experience as humans – or, as Berry says, "the consciousness of the earth and the eventuality of the universe." It is the connecting thread that binds together every moment and every being. It is naturally inherent in every one of us, which makes this five-fold path ever-present and wholly accessible. The only practice we need to access is it is to be human.

Returning to the Cave

In the myth of the weaving at the heart of the world, the tapestry of existence is constantly being made, unmade, and then made again. Every thread that has ever been used is available to us here and now, and every thread that has ever been imagined or dreamed of is also present, waiting to be plucked forward. We must draw up those that will grant us the greatest chance of success, dancing with the uncertainty that we cannot and do not have sole control over the outcomes of our choices. I propose the threads of this five-fold path – Practices, Partners, Plants, Place and Pith – are a solid place from which to begin weaving a collective consciousness that is both entangled with and enchanted by the world in which it evolved.

We need to remember and begin to tell again the old stories of magic and myth and listen to the stories and voices of those we once called and knew as kin. We need stories of forgiveness and deep recollection, ones in which humans and the more-than-human world each hold one key to a door with two locks. "Only stories will help us rejoin *human* to *humility* to *humus*, through their shared root. (The root that we're looking for here is *dhghem*: Earth)" (Powers, 2021, p.76). We need these stories to help us remember where we've come from, to see the pathway laid out, in the liminal space between the spheres, and to start to walk it in earnest. Only through sharing these stories, and walking this path, can we truly (Re)member and (Re)turn.

> The animating language of intuition, alongside the somatically felt senses that relay intuitive knowing to our brains, only exists beyond rationality. We can't simply know or believe the Sacred to be everywhere, we have to feel it in our bones.

Endnotes

[1] Two of the many different sources of this story can be found in Appendix A.

[2] I write "remembering" as "(re)membering" and "returning" as "(re)turning" here and throughout as a reminder that humanity has previously been in the place I am referencing. Separating the word into its constituent parts encourages a reframing of its understanding in this context. What I am suggesting is that we need to re-member ourselves into the animate world and to re-turn into it just as much as we need to remember and return.

References

Abram, D. (2010). *Becoming Animal. An Earthly Cosmology* (1st ed.). Vintage Books.

Abram, D. (1996). *The Spell of the Sensuous: Perception and Language in a More-Than-Human World*. Vintage Books.

Berry, T. (1999). *The Great Work: Our Way into the Future*. Harmony/Bell Tower.

Berry, T., & Swimme, B. (1992). *The Universe Story: From the Primordial Flaring Forth to the Ecozoic Era—A Celebration of the Unfolding of the Cosmos*. Harper San Francisco.

Blackie, S. (2018). The Enchanted Life: Unlocking the Magic of the Everyday. House of Anansi Press.

Bohm, D. (1980). *Wholeness and the Implicate Order*. Routledge. p. 26

Fisher, A. (2014). *Tea Medicine*. Globalteahut.org. pp. 22-23

Hogan, L. (1995). *Dwellings: A Spiritual History of the Living World*. WW Norton.

Gebser, J. (1985). *The Ever-Present Origin*. (N. Barstad & A. Mickunas, Trans.). Ohio University Press. (Original work published 1949)

Meade, M. (Host). (2024, December 11). From Polarization to Re-Creation (No. 413) [Audio podcast episode]. In Living Myth. https://podcasts.apple.com/ca/podcast/living-myth/id1192810215?i=1000680056603

Meade, M. (Host). (2024, November 20). On Hope and Despair (No. 410) [Audio podcast episode]. In Living Myth. https://podcasts.apple.com/ca/podcast/living-myth/id1192810215?i=1000677669778

Meade, M. (2012). *Why the World Doesn't End: Tales of Renewal in Times of Loss* (1st ed.). GreenFire Press.

Merleau-Ponty, M. (2013). *Phenomenology of Perception* (D. Landes, Trans.). Routledge. Original work published 1945)

Parry, G. A. (2015). *Original Thinking: A Radical Revisioning of Time, Humanity, and Nature*. North Atlantic Books.

Powers, R. (2021). A Little More Than Kin. In Van Horn, G., Wall Kimmerer, R., & Hausdoerffer, J. (Eds.). (2021). *Kinship: Belonging in a World of Relations*. Center for Humans and Nature. (pp. 72-79).

Smith, J. E. (Host). (2020, October 20). Noise and the Inner Life [Audio podcast episode]. In *Digital Jung*.

Toben, C. (2023). Thomas Berry on Intuition. *Kosmos: Journal for Global Transformation, 2023*(3). https://www.kosmosjournal.org/kj_article/thomas-berry-on-intuition/

Whyte, D. (1997). *The House of Belonging*. Many Rivers Press.

Zhuangzi. (2009). *The Essential Writing: With Selections from Traditional Commentaries* (B. Ziporyn, Trans.). Hackett Publishing Company Inc.

Appendix A

Two Versions of *The Old Woman in the Cave*

This first version of *The Old Woman in the Cave* is from the White Mountain Apache, as shared in *Why the World Doesn't End,* by Michael Meade (2012).

The old people of the tribes would tell of a special cave where knowledge of the wonders and workings of the world could be found. Even now, some of the native people say that the cave of knowledge exists and might be discovered again. They say it is tucked away on the side of a mountain. "Not too far to go," they say, yet no one seems to find it anymore. Despite all t=he highways and byways, all the thoroughfares and back roads that crosscut the face of the earth, despite all the maps that detail and try to define each area, no one seems to find that old cave. That's too bad, they say, because inside the cave can be found genuine knowledge about how to act when the dark times come around again and the balance of the world tips away from order and slips towards chaos.

Inside the cave, there lives an old woman who remains unaffected by the rush of time and the confusion and strife of daily life. She attends to other things; she has a longer sense of time and a deep capacity for vision. She spends most of her time weaving in the cave where light and shadows play. She wants to fashion the most beautiful garment in the whole world. She has been at this weaving project for a long time and has reached the point of making a fringe for the edge of her exquisitely designed cloak. She wants that fringe to be special; wants it to be meaningful as well as elegant, so she weaves it with porcupine quills. She likes the idea of using something that could poke you as an element of beauty; she likes turning things around and seeing life from odd angles. In order to use the porcupine quills, she must flatten each one with her teeth. After years of biting hard on the quills, her teeth have become worn down to nubs that barely rise above her gums. Still, the old woman keeps biting down and she keeps weaving on.

The only time she interrupts her weaving work is when she goes to stir the soup that simmers in a great cauldron at the back of the cave. The old cauldron hangs over a fire that began a long time ago. The old woman cannot recall anything older than that fire; it just might be the oldest thing there is in this world. Occasionally, she does recall that she must stir the soup that simmers over those flames. For that simmering stew contains all the seeds and roots that become the grains and plants and herbs that sprout up all over the surface of the earth. If the old woman fails to stir the ancient stew once in a while, the fire will scorch the ingredients and there is no telling what troubles might result from that.

So, the old woman divides her efforts between weaving the exquisite cloak and stirring the elemental soup. In a sense, she is responsible for weaving things together as well as for stirring everything up. She senses when the time has come to let the weaving go and stir things up again. Then, she leaves the weaving on the floor of the cave and turns to the task of stirring the soup. Because she is old and tired from her labors and because of the relentless passage of time, she moves slowly, and it takes a while for her to amble over to the cauldron.

As the old woman shuffles across the floor and makes her way to the back of the ancient cave, a black dog watches her every move. The dog was there all along. Seemingly asleep, it awakens as soon as the old weaver turns her attention from one task to the other. As she begins stirring the soup in order to sustain the seeds, the black dog moves to where the weaving lies on the floor of the cave. The dog picks up a loose thread with its teeth and begins pulling on it. As the black dog pulls on the loose thread, the beautiful garment begins to unravel.

Since each thread has been woven to another, pulling upon one begins to undo them all. As the great stew is being stirred up, the elegant garment comes apart and becomes a chaotic mess on the floor.

When the old woman returns to take up her handiwork again, she finds nothing but chaos where there had been a garment of great elegance and beauty. The cloak she has woven with great care has been pulled apart, the fringe all undone; the effort of creation has been turned to naught. The old woman sits and looks silently upon the remnants of her once-beautiful design. She ignores the presence of the black dog as she stares intently at the tangle of undone threads and distorted patterns.

After a while, she bends down, picks up a loose thread, and begins to weave the whole thing again. As she pulls thread after thread from the chaotic mess, she begins again to imagine the most beautiful garment in the whole world. As she weaves, new visions and elegant designs appear before her and her old hands begin to knowingly give them vibrant shape. Soon she has forgotten the cloak she was weaving before as she concentrates on capturing the new design and weaving it into the most beautiful garment ever seen in the world.

This second version of *The Old Woman in the Cave* was shared by Sharon Blackie (2018) in her book *The Enchanted Life: Unlocking the Magic of the Everyday.*

There is an island to the far north-west of these lands, close to the end of the world; you'll maybe have seen it in your dreams. Long white beaches, rocky coves, stormy seas. If you stand on the cliff-tops on its westernmost shores, they say you might sometimes catch a glimpse of Tír na mBan, the Isle of Women, way out on the horizon. When the sky is blue, and the air is still - which happens rarely enough in those parts. Here, the wind blows hard and long through the dark days of winter, and summer is precious and fleeting. Somewhere along the stormiest section of the westernmost coast is a high, inaccessible cave where they say the Old Woman of the World lives still - but no one I've met has ever found that cave, though many have searched, and many have drowned in the process.

No one knows how long she's been in that cave, the Old Woman of the World; she's not even sure herself. She only knows that she doesn't remember having been anywhere else. Are you wondering what she does there? She weaves. You might catch her at it, if you should be lucky enough to happen across that cave - right at the back there, creating an enormous tapestry which she plans will be the most beautiful weaving in the world. Oh, the complexity of it! - and the rainbow colours of the threads, some thick and some thin, some soft, and some shiny. Right now, she's getting ready to make a fringe for the weaving, and she wants the fringe to be as intricate and unique as the body of the tapestry. So, she's making the fringe from sea urchin spines. Because it seems right somehow to the Old Woman of the World that such a beautiful piece of craftsmanship should be finished off by sharp and thorny spines which can sting you if you don't take care. After all - she's weaving the world, and this is the way the world is. She has to flatten the spines to work with them, and so she bites them; and because she has flattened so many of them during the long history of the world, her teeth are little more than stubs.

Over on the other side of the cave is a big fire. They say that the fire has been burning in the cave forever; certainly, the Old Woman can't remember a time when she hasn't tended it. Over that fire hangs an enormous black cauldron, and in that cauldron is a soup which contains all of the seeds and all of the herbs and all of the essence of all of the growing and living things in the world. As well as weaving, it is the Old Woman's job to tend to that soup. But sometimes she gets so caught up in her weaving that she forgets about the soup, and it splutters and splashes - and then she jumps up and crosses to the other side of the cave to stir the pot.

But there's another inhabitant of that cave, and he is biding his time, waiting for the Old Woman to leave her weaving for a moment. He's been watching her, you see - watching all the beautiful shiny threads going back and forth - watching and waiting. He's a big black crow, and his name is Trickster. I wouldn't say that he was a companion to the Old Woman, but wherever she goes he seems to be there too, as if they're bound together somehow, like the weaving and the soup. So, when the Old Woman leaves her loom to tend to the soup, Trickster Crow flies down from his rocky perch at the back of the cave and stands in front of the tapestry.

And then he begins to peck at it. Thread by thread, he begins to unravel it. Faster and faster, picking and pecking, until by the time the Old Woman turns away from the soup and makes her way back to the loom, all that is left is a tangled mess of threads on the floor.

What does the Old Woman do now? Does she weep and wail, sit down by the tangled chaos of her work and grieve because she will never create anything so beautiful again?

She doesn't. Because as she stands there, eyes moist, staring at the mess in front of her, a beautiful rich green thread catches her eye. Who knows why it's that particular thread? But she happens to glance at it, and before she can even begin to think about it, her hands are reaching out and she's picking up that thread and she's weaving it back into the fragments of the warp which remain on her loom - and before she really understands what's happening, a new pattern is already beginning to emerge, and a new tapestry is taking form. And Trickster Crow cackles and caws and flies back to his perch.

The Old Woman isn't thinking about the beautiful work that was lost, or wasting her time getting angry at Trickster Crow, because the Old Woman is a weaver, and weaving is what she does. Weaving is what she is for. So, on she goes, warp and weft, thread after beautiful thread, weaving a new pattern until the next time that the soup needs stirring and Trickster Crow flies down again from his perch. Because Trickster Crow understands this: that if the weaving is ever finished in all its beautiful perfection, the world will come to an end. And so, Trickster keeps on disrupting, and the Old Woman keeps on weaving through all the ages of the world, so that new patterns are always in the process of becoming, and the end of the world is held at bay for a few ages more.

Appendix B

The Legend of Shennong

They say that long, long ago there lived a great scholar, wiser and older than the cragged mountains he dwelled upon. Many feared him and stayed away... some went to him for advice... and when the people needed advice, they would elect a group of representatives to make the journey up into the mountain and seek out his advice, for whatever else he was, he was their emperor, Shen Nong... One young monk was said to have spent an entire season with Shen Nong on his mountain.... During the colder months [they] would boil herbal drinks.

It was maybe during one such night, possibly when the moon was full and the sky clear, that they sat in the forest listening to the mountain and the sound of the water boiling on a nearby fire. A breeze stirred...Was it chance? Did destiny reach out and pluck the leaf from the tree and, in the form of wind, let it fall into the boiling water below? Who can say? But Shen Nong was never one to question the gifts of nature... and after a few bowls, the Sage exclaimed the legendary words that are carved in the rock and brushed to paper, inspiring us even today. "This is the emperor of all medicinal herbs." (Fisher, 2014, pp. 22-23).

Fascist America or Sacred America: The Choice is Ours

Glenn Aparicio Parry

When a man unprincipled in private life … bold in his temper…—despotic in his ordinary demeanour—known to have scoffed in private at the principles of liberty—when such a man is seen to mount the hobby horse of popularity—to join in the cry of danger to liberty—to take every opportunity of embarrassing the General Government & bringing it under suspicion—to flatter and fall in with all the nonsense of the zealots of the day—It may justly be suspected that his object is to throw things into confusion that he may ride the storm and direct the whirlwind. (Alexander Hamilton in Remnick, 2019)

This is a time of great uncertainty in America. The world order was upended in the first weeks of the new administration. Long-term alliances were undone while cozying up to long-term enemies. Tariffs were placed on nearly 100 countries, with the glaring exception of Russia and Belarus. The on again and off again tariffs were terrifying to almost everyone. Wild fluctuations in the stock market have induced anxiety, if not outright panic, over what the future might bring. A recession seems inevitable, if not a depression, or a world war. Why make international trade so unpredictable and unstable? Does Trump really believe tariffs will be beneficial or is something else afoot? I suspect the latter.

In times like these, the words of Alexander Hamilton quoted above come to mind. Trump is a trickster figure intentionally sowing chaos so that he may direct the whirlwind and consolidate power. He has already installed sycophants into positions of power. He has significantly eroded the justice system, and many of his executive orders—such as putting an end to birthright citizenship—basically ignored the Constitution. People are being deported without due process, including green card holders and those on student visas. The president has sought to withhold funds from universities, including Harvard, and also from law firms who assisted the prosecution in the January 6th insurrection case against him that was suspended after he won reelection.

> For the first fifty years of our nation's history, the entire world recognized the United States as a hybrid of Native American and Euro-American cultures.

One of the first steps Trump and his unelected conspirator Elon Musk took was to eliminate the watchdogs within government, firing the very people responsible for investigating fraud and abuse (Inspector Generals) under the pretext of eliminating fraud and abuse. Musk left his full-time role, but the man who hired him remains. The same man who has been convicted multiple times of fraud in both civil and criminal court has somehow hoodwinked his base into believing he is the one most suited to clean up corruption in the so-called deep state.

The first Trump administration was a

Glenn Aparicio Parry, is a Nautilus award-winning author of *Original Thinking: A Radical Revisioning of Time, Humanity, and Nature* (North Atlantic Press, 2015), *Original Politics: Making America Sacred Again* (SelectBooks, 2020), the first two thirds of the trilogy that preceded *Original Love: The Timeless Source of Wholeness* (Select Books, 2026). The founder and past president of the SEED Institute, Parry is currently an adjunct faculty member of the California Institute of Integral Studies, the president of the think tank: Circle for Original Thinking, and the host of the Circle for Original Thinking podcast. https://glennaparicioparry.com

little like this—chaotic and seemingly out of control. But there were "adults in the room" then (people like General Mattis, HR McMaster, and chief economic advisor Gary Cohn) who successfully restrained the worst instincts of the president, at least for a while. However, by the end of the first term, it was obvious that the guardrails protecting democracy were disintegrating.

The Long View of American History

In my book *Original Politics: Making America Sacred Again,* published in 2020, I began a chapter called *Fascist America or Sacred America* with these words:

> I have said that America is on an inexorable path toward realizing its original sacred purpose of unity in diversity. I believe America—the place and nation—will return to that sacred purpose again. I admit to another possibility, however: one in which America rejects its destiny and devolves in the opposite direction so far it cannot right the ship. …America could become a fascist state. In truth, both possibilities have been in play ever since we broke away from monarchy and began our experimental path forward. Today, a fascist America seems more possible than ever before; yet, at the same time, the seeds of a sacred America are still present. (Parry, 2020, p. 217)

To understand why both a sacred or fascist America is in play it is necessary to take a long view of United States history. The colonists lived in close proximity to Native Americans for 150 years before they chose to break away from their mother country of England to establish a new nation. During that century and a half, the settlers had ample opportunity to observe Native American governance, which was truly egalitarian. The core values of the young nation—liberty, equality, and natural rights—were all profoundly influenced by, if not directly appropriated from Native American values.

For the first fifty years of our nation's history, the entire world recognized the United States as a hybrid of Native American and Euro-American cultures.

It was only after Andrew Jackson came into power in the late 1820s and began a century long reign of terror on Native America that the memory of such influence was nearly totally erased.

In the past half century, a number of researchers: Oren Lyons (1992), John Mohawk (1992), Bruce Johansen and Donald Grinde (1991), Sally Roesch Wagner (2001), Betty Booth Donahoe (2020), and Stephen Sachs (2020), to name a few, have sought to reestablish a revisionist history of America that properly acknowledges Native influence on the founding fathers. The US Government explicitly acknowledged this truth during the 1980s, making a resolution honoring Indian Nations for their influence:

> Be it resolved by the Senate (The House of Representatives concurring) that the Congress on the occasion of the 200th anniversary of the signing of the US Constitution, acknowledges the historical debt which the Republic of the USA owes to the Iroquois Confederacy and other Indian Nations for their demonstrations of enlightened, democratic principles of government and their example of a free association of Independent Indian Nations. (http://www.oneidaindiannation.com/haudenosaunee-impact-recognized-by-congress/).

In truth, Native influence on our core values and founding documents was even stronger than acknowledged in the 1980s. Native influence was the primary inspiration for the original founding document that preceded the US Constitution: *The Articles of Confederation.* The principal writer of the Articles was Benjamin Franklin, who drew heavily upon The Iroquois (Haudenosaunee) Great Law of Peace in crafting the document. Franklin, who became friends with Chief

Canasatego when he was Indian Ambassador to the Haudenosaunee during the French and Indian Wars, closely modeled the Articles after the Indian practice of community service. All politicians served a limited term and received no compensation or emoluments of any kind. The Articles were the law of the land from 1781—when France and Morocco recognized the United States as a country after the Articles of Confederation were ratified—until 1789, when the US Constitution supplanted it.

Most of us are unaware that under the Articles of Confederation there were presidents, at least in name. These proto-presidents held a much different, less powerful role than today, serving a one-year term that was largely ceremonial. Historians rightly distinguish these early presidents from those that came after because they essentially held little power. Yet that is precisely the main

> It is important to realize that the nation has been ceding power to the presidency from the start, beginning with the changeover from the Articles of Confederation to the US Constitution.

point I wish to convey in this paper: *We began as far away from monarchy as possible. We have been ceding more and more power to the presidency ever since.*

The US Constitutional Convention: A Shift Toward Greater Presidential Powers

At the Constitutional Convention, two plans emerged: the New Jersey Plan that proposed relatively modest changes to the Articles of Confederation, and the Virginia plan that proposed much bolder changes. The New Jersey plan retained a legislature of just one chamber with each state having one vote, and in lieu of a president, it proposed an executive council with all voices heard equally.

The Virginia Plan was not a revision as much as a new document. Its salient features included a system of checks and balances provided through the articulation of three distinct branches of government: executive, legislative, and judicial;

it also proposed a bi-cameral legislature (the House and Senate). Significantly, the proposal called for a legislature with proportional representation depending upon state population and a much stronger executive—a president with a seven-year term—a huge departure from the one-year presidency defined under the Articles of Confederation. The Virginia Plan also proposed that the Federal government have the power to tax the people in order to build a common defense against foreign enemies. In fact, the Virginia Plan represented a dramatic restart of the republic with a significantly enlarged role for the federal government, the president, and a corresponding diminishment of state powers. (Chernow, 2005)

As these two plans were being debated, Hamilton made a passionate and long-winded speech in which he envisioned a hybrid form of government that had the continuity of a monarchy combined with the liberties of a republic; the president could continue to serve indefinitely provided he embodied "good behavior." Hamilton's intent was to guard against anarchy and tyranny alike, and he distinguished his form of monarchy from its European counterparts by referring to the president as an "elected monarch."[1] William Samuel Johnson quipped that Hamilton's speech was "praised by everybody [and]…supported by none," but in actuality four states voted in favor of Hamilton's proposal of "good behavior," including the delegation from Virginia that included James Madison. Madison even proposed that the federal government be given the power to veto any state laws "as the King of Great Britain heretofore had." Franklin and others strongly opposed a presidential or federal veto, for this smacked of monarchy, and they wanted nothing that too closely resembled that from which they had just broken away. Hamilton, chastened by those in attendance, never again uttered a kind word about monarchy, "elected" or otherwise other than to caution against it. (Chernow, p 231-232).

While the idea of an "elected monarch" was seemingly expunged from American history, the truth is it did not disappear from the American psyche. There has always been a faction of the

nation somewhat uncomfortable with the radical nature of the American experiment. Today, nearly two and a half centuries after Hamilton made his speech at the Constitutional convention, the idea for an American monarch is making a surprising comeback.

The History of Ceding Power to the Presidency

It is important to realize that the nation has been ceding power to the presidency from the start, beginning with the changeover from the Articles of Confederation to the US Constitution. The presidency was given far greater power at that time, but such concession of powers did not stop there. The executive branch has been accruing power ever since.

The checks and balances of the US Constitution were well conceived, but many of the checks against the executive branch have proven ineffective over time. Consider impeachment. While several presidents have been impeached, none have ever been convicted by the Senate, including Trump, who was impeached twice in his first term, the second time for fomenting an insurrection against his own government. Only Congress is supposed to declare war, but the last time that happened was 1942. Since WWII, presidents have skirted the law, waging war in Korea, Vietnam, Iraq, Afghanistan, and elsewhere, while Congress has stood idly by.

Many Americans are aghast at what is currently transpiring. The executive branch is aggressively usurping power from both the legislative and judicial branches, and neither Congress nor the Supreme Court are taking steps to reassert the authority of their own branches. Americans are wondering: Why is this happening today?

What we are currently witnessing is the culmination of a half century long effort from the conservative think tank The Heritage Foundation (founded in

1973) to implement a "unitary executive," in which nearly all governmental power would be transferred to the executive branch. The "Mandate for Leadership" of Project 2025 first appeared in 1981 under the same name at the beginning of the Reagan administration (Goza, 2024). In the opening pages of the Project 2025 document, its current leaders openly acknowledge the lineage that connects them to the Reagan administration. It was under Reagan that the nation not only began a shift toward enhanced power of the presidency, but also a rapid

We began as far away from monarchy as possible. We have been ceding more and more power to the presidency ever since.

turn toward income inequality, with top tier income tax rates being cut from 70% to 33%, and further protections enacted to limit inheritance taxes, ensuring intergenerational wealth.

The Heritage Foundation went on to become the most influential arm of the Republican Party in Supreme Court nominations, which led to the 2010 Citizens United decision that opened the floodgates of unlimited corporate money in politics. The Heritage Foundation was also instrumental in bringing about the controversial decision granting legal immunity to the president for official acts. The sum total of all of these actions has been to set the stage for an authoritarian takeover of government. In short, we cannot simply blame Trump for the current predicament we are now in. If not him, someone else would have come along to take advantage of the situation.

As soon as the Trump administration ends in disgrace, while the embers of the charred republic are still warm, we need a second Constitutional convention. A truth and reconciliation commission is not enough. There must be a convention with the express purpose of protecting against the abuses of power that have occurred in the past 50 years that have dismantled the checks and balances that were intended by our founders. Among the many actions I might envision, the Supreme Court must be completely revamped, with no Justices enjoying lifetime appointments and some basic rules for ethical conduct established, overseen by a committee composed of emeritus and emerita members of the Congress and Supreme Court. The immunity decision clearly must be reversed and the tenet that nobody is above the law, not even the president, reaffirmed. Moreover, the current Department of Justice practice prohibiting indictment of a sitting president must also be rescinded; even a sitting president must be able to be prosecuted if they are egregiously ignoring the law. Congress must also no longer give presidents a blank check for war powers, reasserting their Constitutional authority as the only branch empowered to declare war. And if Congress establishes a department, such as the Department of Education or the Environmental Protection Agency, there should be reasonable limits as to how much the executive branch can restructure the agency. Any government department or agency that has been legally established by an act of Congress should not be cut by more than 15% (or some other reasonable agreed upon percentage) during any one term of the presidency. Finally, and perhaps most importantly, the 2010 Citizens United Supreme Court decision must be overturned, for as soon as unlimited corporate contributions became possible, the imposition of an oligarchy became inevitable. All these changes and more must be done to ensure the reconstitution and continuation of a representational republic that, despite its faults, was once the envy of all democracies throughout the free world.

References

Chernow, R. (2005). *Alexander Hamilton.* New York, Penguin.

Parry, G. A. (2020). *Original Politics: Making America Sacred Again,* Berkeley, Ca. Select-Books.

Lyons, Chief O., & Mohawk, J., editors. (1992). *Exiled in the Land of the Free: Democracy, Indian Nations and the US Constitution.* Santa Fe. Clear Light Publishers.

Grinde, D., & Johansen, B. (1991). *Exemplar of Liberty: Native America and the Evolution of Democracy.* Los Angeles. American Indian Studies Center.

Roesch Wagner, S. (2001). *Sisters in Spirit: Haudenosaunee (Iroquois) Influence on Early American Feminists.* Summertown, Tn. Native Voices .

Remnick, D. (2019). "The Sober Clarity of the Impeachment Witnesses." *New Yorker,* November 15.

Sachs, S. (2020). Editor *Honoring the Circle: Ongoing Learning of the West from American Indians on Politics and Society.* Cardiff by the Sea, Ca. Waterside Productions.

Goza, J. E. (2024). Los Angeles Times, Opinion. August 25. https://www.latimes.com/opinion/story/2024-08-25/project-2025-trump-heritage-foundation-election

The Butterfly's Congregation
by Chun Yu

What a chance it is
for a group of strangers
to gather around a tiny creature
blind, immobile, and concealed
a chrysalis under an ordinary leaf
on the side of a hidden path:

A divorced young mother
with a little boy, too afraid
to carry her phone to take photos
in fear of her ex-husband's
stalking

A middle-aged man
snuck away from his job
holding a heavy camera
guarding what he discovered
hours a time for three weeks

An outlander
left her dream behind
trampled like broken wings
wandering across the ocean

Yet, the chrysalis has a beaded rim
the leaf's edge a golden glimmer
and we each carries hopes and
　　dreams
secret, blind, and unstated
but couldn't help to glow

What a chance it is
to come together
as who we are—

watching the life
hidden, coiled, and pressed
under a thousand folds
breaking and bursting
into the world
we each whisper:

"It is I!"
"It is I!"
"It is I!"

The new butterfly
fully opened into its being
suddenly takes off
without a blink of eyes
to the blue blue sky
leaving us—
the butterfly's congregation
looking up
into the sky with no edge
and sing together:

"It is I!"
"It is I!"
"It is I!"

Chun Yu, Ph.D. is an award-winning bilingual (English and Chinese) poet, graphic novelist, scientist, and translator. She is the author of a memoir in verse "Little Green: Growing Up During the Chinese Cultural Revolution" (Simon & Schuster) winning multiple awards, and a historical graphic novel in progress (Macmillan), and more. Her poetry and stories have been published or are forthcoming in the Boston Herald, Orion, Poetry Northwest, Arion Press, MIT Tech Talk, Xinhua Daily, Poem of the Day (San Francisco Public Library), Heyday Books, and more. Her work is taught in world history and culture classes in the U.S. and internationally. Chun is an honoree of YBCA 100 award (2020) for creative changemakers. She has been awarded grants from San Francisco Arts Commission, Zellerbach, Poets & Writers, Sankofa Fund, and more. Chun holds a B.S. and M.S. from Peking University and a Ph.D. from Rutgers University. She was a post-doctoral fellow in a Harvard-MIT joint program.

The Living Heart of the Constitution

Barbara (Be) Scott

On November 6, 2024, I woke up at 3 a.m. with a post-election-night hangover—and I don't even drink. Like millions of other Americans, I made it through that day but honestly do not remember how. For the first time in my civic life, I felt there was nothing we could do to stop the destruction of our country.

Then a second thought overtook the first—that we shouldn't even try, at least not yet. At this juncture, no amount of plotting and strategizing could be effective. The words "wait," "trust," and "watch" spoke themselves to me that morning, and I fell back on the teachings of the *Tao te Ching,* which I tend to do in times of uncertainty, remembering the question Lao Tzu posed roughly 2,500 years ago: "Do you have the patience to wait / till your mud settles and the water is clear? / Can you remain unmoving /

Barbara Scott (Be) lives in Taos, New Mexico. She earned a master of liberal arts degree from the Graduate Institute at St. John's College in 2012. She started her business, Final Eyes, in Denver, Colorado, working since 1981 in the fields of publishing and design. She has written many op-ed pieces for *The Taos News* under the names Barbara Scott and Be Scott, and she published a worldview journal, *Threshold of the Millennium,* in 1992. The journal was intended to be used as a way to track significant changes, across twelve categories, in the last decade of the last millennium. She can be reached at finaleyes@icloud.com.

till the right action arises by itself?" (Mitchell, 2015).

I had always maintained that Americans were inherently decent. I still believe that; but those who have succumbed to the onslaught of lies and conspiracies are no longer themselves: they have taken on the words, character, and behavior of their propagandists. Hannah Arendt spoke to this idea in reference to dictators who succeeded in "contaminating their subjects with the specifically totalitarian virus" (Arendt, 1951). But in this era of social media, with its instant posts and reposts; 24-hour cable news networks devoted to destroying democracy; and nonstop talking heads on all forms of media regurgitating and amplifying those lies, Donald Trump was able to tap into a messaging zeitgeist that was unfathomable in the time of Hitler, Mussolini, or Stalin.

So it came as a sickening revelation that goodness in this country might never again be seen as a shared value, unless it could be passed naturally from one person to another, face to face, through simple trust based on each individual's authenticity and sincerity. I felt immediately prompted to physically gather with others who would be interested in creating more trusting and truthful relationships. Before engaging in any political action, we needed to heal our hearts from what felt like betrayal by our fellow citizens. I drafted an invitation and posted it on Facebook, the gist of which was this:

Let's not separate from each other by going too deeply inward at this time. And seriously, let's break away from the bad news. Connecting one on one with people we both know and don't know seems like one solution. ... The first six people who RSVP via FB Messenger are invited to my house at 7 p.m. next Tuesday night for a heartwarming party.

Five days later, nine people turned up at my house for the inaugural get-togeth-

"

er. We did not discuss strategy, politics, or how to win the next round. In fact, we agreed not to speak of the election. We each shared our personal stories, and we all listened carefully. We laughed with each other and felt sorrow at times; we grew closer by revealing something deeply personal about ourselves. We did not bond through common cause but by simple acceptance of one another.

A week or two later, a woman I was just getting to know through the Unitarian Congregation of Taos—another lifeline that lifted me and others from despair—emailed to ask for some information about the heartwarming gatherings. I explained the impetus and invited her and her husband to come. She responded: "Fantastic, Be, every last little bit of it. Sometimes it is the simple act of community witnessing—joy, acts of kindness, happiness. At this point joy feels positively and deliciously subversive."

By our third meeting, everyone was struggling with the debasement of our nation: They were concerned for all the federal workers who'd lost their jobs

cism, and sovereignty. One guest read the words of Nobel Prize-winning chemist Ilya Prigogine, suggesting we make them our bywords: "When a complex system is far from equilibrium, small islands of coherence in a sea of chaos have the capacity to shift the entire system to a higher order."[1]

Sovereignty: An Inalienable Birthright

That gathering prompted me to think more deeply about our Constitution, starting with the word sovereignty, not just as a political term of self-governance, but as a principle of being individuals who are whole and complete in themselves, free to rule themselves according to their own values as long as they didn't impinge on others' rights. Although the entire Constitution is devoted to the idea of sovereignty, the word never appears in the Preamble, the Bill of Rights, or the body of the Constitution itself. But the unspoken idea is present throughout. Our country is sovereign, but so are we, as citizens of a sovereign nation. In the case of the United States, it means

attend church…or not, whom to marry and whether to have children. Thomas Paine, one of the most provocative of the Founding Fathers, stated this tendency to undervalue the precious in his essay "The American Crisis," which he wrote as a soldier during the American Revolution, in 1776:

What we obtain too cheap, we esteem too lightly: it is dearness only that gives every thing its value. Heaven knows how to put a proper price upon its goods; and it would be strange indeed if so celestial an article as *Freedom* should not be highly rated.

We seldom thought to fully appreciate freedom of choice and the rule of law. But now we are faced with Project 2025, which envisions the establishment of a dictator as the Christian nationalist boss, rather than a republic with a "democratically" elected president and an elected body of representatives. (If you don't count the electoral college and legally permitted gerrymandering, we could use democratically without putting it in quotes.)

While we can all agree that the country has never been perfect and has at times exercised brutality, the promise to change the things that aren't perfect has always just required a majority of citizens to want them to change badly enough that they would press their representatives in Congress to legislate that change, as they have done so many times. But we must face the reality that not every American is onboard with moving forward. Some would rather go back to simpler, more homogeneous times. Project 2025 is the roadmap for that regression.

Even before the Project 2025 plot to strip Americans of their basic rights, most of us were aware of the dangers to this nation. It's hard to imagine that average U.S. citizens have ever spent as much time and money in an effort to avert those dangers as they did in the last three elections—on both sides of the political divide. It's a big responsibility for an individual to feel like the fate of the nation rests on their involvement and their endless donations to particular candidates. But because of Citizens United, the 2010 Supreme Court decision granting corporations the right to donate enormous amounts of money to a

> "In free governments, the rulers are the servants and the people their superiors and sovereigns." *(Benjamin Franklin)*

in Elon Musk's cruel rampage against civil servants. Trump was threatening to make a deal with Israel to buy the Gaza Strip and turn it into a luxury resort. And USAID (the United States Agency for International Development) had been gutted, halting billions of dollars in aid to suffering people around the world. These were just three of the many outrages brought up that night. We tried to keep it personal—how does it affect my heart, my mind—without tail-spinning into rants about the recklessness we were all witnessing. I reminded everyone that these get-togethers had not been initiated to discuss politics, but when political actions trickle down to make us viscerally miserable, here was a place to share those feelings in an accepting circle of understanding and compassion.

When the agonized sharing was over, we had a discussion about love, fas-

entirely in union—sovereign individuals within sovereign states as part of a sovereign nation—choosing to be as one. Benjamin Franklin described it this way: "In free governments, the rulers are the servants and the people their superiors and sovereigns." This concept, defined as popular sovereignty, refers to government powers that issue from the people to their representatives—in every facet of political life, all the way from a city council to the U.S. presidency. (For a broader discussion on sovereignty, especially as it relates to Native Americans, see Júrgen W. Kremer's article, "There Always Has Been an Alternate Story," in this issue.)

In our naïveté, or perhaps complacency, ordinary Americans had considered inevitable and everlasting the simple freedoms of self-determination, such as where to settle, work, go to college,

single candidate or party, the individual's donations are a cruel joke. To wit, Elon Musk paid nearly $300 million to help Donald Trump and other Republican Party candidates take over this country. No doubt he would have paid more, considering the power those payments have purchased, not to mention access to even more wealth through government contracts that he is now in a position to rewrite entirely in his own favor.

Despite our burden of responsibility not to bury our heads in the sand, many of us have found it too sickening to watch the ongoing sadistic depredations, such as the firing of thousands of civil servants, many of whose lives and the lives of their families will be forever altered. In the main, the quick dismantlement of the federal bureaucracy (including USAID, the largest mitigator of human suffering in the world) seems intended to signal the extent of our powerlessness. The alliance with Vladimir Putin and Russia; the bullying dismissal of a democratic ally, Ukraine; and Trump's March 4 speech to Congress, in which the leader of the free world taunted his opponents and told lie after lie in a voice meant to mesmerize his followers into even more strident obsequiousness, have all had the effect of throwing the rest of us off balance. When nothing makes sense and there's no time to adjust to each new travesty, it's like objects moving in space when you expect them to remain still: the effect is dizziness, with the tendency to sit it out until the nausea passes.

These forces have wasted no time unfurling a hateful agenda, displacing the stars and stripes with a dystopian vision that will strip us of what had always felt like an inalienable birthright. And which, actually, *is* an inalienable birthright.

A Brief History of a Revolutionary Idea

Personally, I would feel like I was betraying the Founding Fathers if I did not cross my own Delaware to protect the Constitution and its Bill of Rights, documents that have persisted through time for 238 and 234 years respectively, making each of our private and public lives far better than they ever would have been without them. Even though the Constitution has both ruptured and

mended in ways, it still bears within its heart the catalyst of progress and revolution.

In the Preamble to the Constitution, its most fundamental words are ones every schoolchild learns: "We the People…" That simple phrase undeniably bestows the benefits of the ensuing words on each and every one of us, no matter our socioeconomic or political status, our race, religion, or sexual orientation.

It even promises those rights to those who may not yet have been granted them, because that is the vision—that every single person be left alone to live freely—and sometimes even to be aided in that endeavor.

Beyond the substance, our fervent *belief* in those words has given them almost infinite power. In fact, most American citizens have not even read the Constitution, but many know by heart at least fragments of its Preamble, the remainder of which is a brief continuation, stating its radical vision in a single sentence:

We the People of the United States, in Order to form a more perfect Union, establish Justice, insure domestic Tranquility, provide for the common defence, promote the general Welfare, and secure the Blessings of Liberty to ourselves and our Posterity, do ordain and establish this Constitution for the United States of America.

The phrase "We the People" bestows these blessings, but it also imposes responsibility on those selfsame people. Long have we relied on our government to do a job we ourselves must now undertake. For our role model, we can look to one of the unsung Founding Fathers, Gouverneur Morris, the very man who finalized the language of the

Constitution and took the personal liberty of rewriting the Preamble to affirm some of his moral arguments that had been rejected, mostly by slaveholders, on the floor of the Pennsylvania State-house in Philadelphia in just under four months in 1787.[2]

Chosen by the delegates for his admirable thinking and writing skills, Morris was said to have the capacity to hold big ideas. Gouverneur was not a title but his first name, after his mother's maiden name. Perhaps this is why it seemed natural for him to value the opinions of women, which he rather famously did, because, in a deviation from the patriarchal norm, he was named for his mother, not his father. Gouverneur (most think his name was pronounced "governor") was a tall, imposing man. At the age of 28, his ankle was crushed beneath the wheel of an open carriage. The injury required amputation of the leg below the knee, which may account at least in part for his great empathy in the face of human suffering.

And while the words he wrote may not have the legal utility required for a court case, they do have the moral authority that supports every kind of legislation that pertains to the values it denotes. Knowing that this brief statement has found its way into the fiber of nearly every citizen's being reveals that Morris could be considered a radical for his times—not in the "unruly change at any cost" terms but under this definition: "marked by a considerable departure from the usual or traditional." Perhaps because of his respect for women and his empathy for those who suffered, he believed in natural rights and envisioned equality and civil rights for all. Outspoken on the floor of what would later be known as Independence Hall, he was well-liked among the other delegates because while he had strong opinions and made them known, he also knew how to bring levity to the serious arguments under debate. More important, he could poke fun at himself. If people can't help but laugh with you, they are much more inclined to listen to you and tolerate your opinions.

After the Constitution's details were fully agreed upon, Morris, as a member of the Committee of Style and Arrangement, was selected to give the document its final language. The document already

momentum; but opposite and equal forces—such as caring, unselfishness, activism, and love for one's fellow human beings—freed and propelled it.

Morris applied two of his gifts—visionary thinking and the power of the pen—to rewrite the Preamble to also indicate that the Constitution's purpose was to form a more perfect Union—not a confederation of 13 states, as in the original version. It was almost a spiritual statement, a union meaning "One," while 13 had exemplified separation. It was as if Morris understood nonduality

dom, justice, and the rule of law (not of man) as something to be treasured and safeguarded, even—and especially—by individual citizens. When those citizens vote, regardless of party affiliation, they are taking that responsibility seriously, and in their minds, they are preserving our way of life and the country's values.

The problem is only that we citizens don't agree on the values most worth preserving. The discrepancy is one of scale. Some think the privileges they enjoy can be scaled up and enjoyed by all. Even those who are not citizens, for instance, might expect to receive due process, if not common decency and compassion. Others see the scaling up of rights and privileges for those who differ from them as a fundamental diminishment of their own. We all appreciate roughly the same set of rights. It's just a matter of who should lay claim to those rights.

Though we have more than enough work to do on ourselves as citizens, the Constitution is still very much in place, despite wishful thinking by the Trump administration and Project 2025 conspirators. A few examples of the progress we can look back on, and feel proud of, include the following:

> Our ongoing reverence for this founding document can guide us to the full realization that it literally has been and must continue to be "We the People" who constitute America and who continue to manifest its vision.

had a sort of introductory paragraph, which briefly discussed the 13 states and how they would govern themselves. It did the job but was uninspired:

> We the People of the States of New-Hampshire, Massachusetts, Rhode-Island and Providence Plantations, Connecticut, New-York, New-Jersey, Pennsylvania, Delaware, Maryland, Virginia, North-Carolina, South-Carolina, and Georgia—do ordain, declare and establish the following Constitution for the Government of Ourselves and our Posterity.[3]

It must also have seemed to Morris insufficiently visionary. So, taking the kind of liberty he imagined for the rest of the country, he rewrote it—not just as a statement of purpose but as a statement of vision. And it is within this Preamble to the Constitution that a perpetual-motion idea was planted by the man who firmly believed in equal rights *for all.*

Like all heavenly bodies, in which forces like gravity and electromagnetism both propel and drag on the object in motion, the Constitution was subjected to forces like greed, self-entitlement, racism, sexism, and a hunger for power, each of which acted to slow its

and the underlying consciousness that unifies us all. And perhaps he did.

Miraculously, it seems, no one insisted on changes to the language he had penned, and it was left alone with its coiled spring of vision intact. Not only did it lay the foundation for a more perfect Union, but it went on to unimaginable lengths to endow U.S. citizens with all the blessings we have come to take for granted—radical, transformative ambitions, like freedom and justice for all. Does that sound like a cliché now? Maybe that's why it's under such grave threat, because we grew complacent and relied too much on the government to protect and assert those rights, rather than regard them as the precious life-giving force that we the people bear the responsibility to value and preserve.

Our country—our still imperfect Union: At almost 250 years as a steady democratic republic, we had come to regard America not as perfect but at least as an exemplar of fair and decent governance—of choice and opportunity. We view our forefathers in an almost mythological light. We see that they were human beings with flaws, but we also recognize the dedication with which they articulated their lofty ideals of free-

- Slavery is no longer legal; African Americans have the right to live, work, vote, and own property wherever they wish. These rights ultimately extended to citizens in all ethnic and racial minority groups.
- The U.S. Army and American pioneers in search of land are no longer killing with impunity indigenous populations, who were here long before the Europeans and British arrived.
- Women, once treated as their husband's property, enjoy the same rights as men: They vote, hold property, borrow money, and have legal rights of personhood in marriage as well as in divorce and custody disputes. For a time, they even possessed the biological right to their own bodies, until the Supreme Court—dominated by six conservative Catholics—transferred those rights to the states, where they were usurped by the privilege of states' rights. This judicial activism has long-term repercussions for women

and girls that hark back to slavery—meaning bondage and performance of services at the will of another without compensation.

- Children, once considered the property of their fathers, have over the years been granted rights of protection, opportunity, and even, in certain cases, emancipation.
- Same-sex and multiracial marriage have both become legal in the last 60 years.
- Disabled people have won—over many, many years—access to equal rights under the law.

All of these vitally beneficial changes in the lives of citizens have issued forth from the Constitution, which provided the legal but also the moral basis for human transformation. But we must admit that it was the will and the vision of "the people" themselves—a free people, unified with the vision and backing of the Constitution—who ignited that engine of change. It has always been the people who carried forth the Constitution's promissory mission to include *every citizen* in that vision. As disability-rights activist Lawrence Carter-Long stated: "Race, gender, ethnicity, age, sexuality: People had to claw and scratch and fight and protest and pass legislation in order for those things to get recognized as valid!"

It took a while for us to understand the full implications of where this brilliant document could take us. But its seeds had been planted, and their possibilities had begun to germinate in the minds and spirits of those who were compassionate enough to allow them to take root in their souls. The people who fought for the legislation that brought about these advances in human rights over the next 200-plus years were regular citizens who could not tolerate witnessing the injustices of *their* day, let alone perpetuate them. People, *the* people, have acted as the living voice of the Constitution for all of these ensuing years, protesting in the streets, on buses, and in government buildings in order to work through inequity after profound inequity. The goal in most cases could be distilled to a very simple idea: *the acceptance and allowance of people as they are.*

We are living in the human world. It is not equal, and it is not just. We merely had a virtuous citizenry that took its direction from the vision of its primary guide on self-governance, the Constitution. And legislators, who listened to and represented the people's interests and will, enacted laws in response to the injustices that remained. Still, we must remind ourselves: their power to do so issued entirely from the people who elected them.

Our ongoing reverence for this founding document can guide us to the full realization that it literally has been and must continue to be "We the People" who constitute America and who continue to manifest its vision. Those who care about the rights of others have tapped into something mystical: a hidden clause within the Preamble itself that continues to spin an invisible mechanism designed to fully realize for everyone what had only been idealized by the founders, and only for white men: true freedom—for all of us. What was that hidden clause? Not hidden, but not yet revealed as the churning force inside the document that would instill its own internal sense of fairness and progress on future citizens. What was it in the Constitution that both generated this ongoing revolution and insisted upon it for almost a quarter of a millennium?

but rather the seeds of perfection, which have continued to bear fruit for all these many years. The contention is between trusting the Constitution and doubting its power. After all, it is a work of man, not of God. Although sometimes it has certainly felt and acted like the work of God.

At some level, knowing that our government is no longer there to ensure just and fair results, it is challenging for all of us at some level to think that the Constitution can endure and continue to work its alchemy. In fact, the current government intends to put as swift an end to it as possible. But they have not reckoned with visionary power, for which raw power is no match. To accept that it is our civic duty to protect this country—to make sure the vision of its constitution survives—might sound impractical at best. But to underestimate the inherent power vested in the people is to underestimate how deeply its promise is rooted within our very psyche—as individuals and as a nation. That promise will not easily relinquish itself, if at all. We need to trust in its seemingly auto-volitional, perhaps mystical, force. If we truly care about what was set out in the Preamble, then we need to promise each other to preserve it by living its values until the

> By *being* the Constitution, by living its values in public every single day without fail, we can choose to be transformed by living from our hearts and caring for our fellow citizens and for those who wish to be citizens.

Inarguably, the most important idea was embedded in the first three words of the Preamble, "We the People," which placed us all on equal footing, without even a suggestion of hierarchy. But equally potent in its visionary capacity was the perpetual motion created by the infinitive of the verb 'to form.' *"To form a more perfect union"* does not specify some end to that ongoing process, but the opposite. The achievement of perfection can never be complete, so inside the document itself lay not imperfection

time when all Americans are once again prepared to cherish it.

How do we carry forward the values and work of the Constitution without a government to protect and enforce it? The answer is that *we must BE the constitution.* We the People constitute America. Those of us who studied civics, who have read the Constitution, and who learned to treasure the gifts we were born to think of as God-given entitlements, must take a leadership role in helping other Americans see how essential we all are as we move ahead into what feels like another revolutionary war.

As someone who has studied different versions of the *Tao te Ching* for many years, I've become fairly skilled at letting go. But letting go of the ugly is much easier than letting go of the beautiful. Releasing a stance of protectiveness toward our Constitution and the promise of true democracy would be extremely painful—if that's what I intended to do. But I do not intend to let it go. Even if it's wrenched from us, we will reclaim it by whatever means necessary, because the Constitution is not just a parchment document hanging in the National Archives: it is instilled in our very DNA, an epigenetic phenomenon influenced by living every day as a free person, even if we did take it for granted; by stories of our ancestors living as free people every day of their lives, or, for those who still remain outside its blessings, knowing that its promise is not yet fulfilled—but only because of human flaws, not shortcomings of the document itself.

The Constitution was and still is the guiding star to what we consider the full potential of liberty and equality for all. We are all in the field of sovereignty, and we all belong. By *being* the Constitution, by living its values in public every single day without fail, we can choose to be transformed by living from our hearts and caring for our fellow citizens and for those who wish to be citizens.

I believe that one of the great existential purposes of the United States is to prove to itself and the world that love actually works. Love, in political terms, means just what those who are currently in power have turned their explosive self-entitlement on: Diversity, Equity, and Inclusion for all people, not just straight white males and not just those born into wealth, power, and privilege. This country has shown for many generations that politics *is* love. Otherwise, why would Americans—both citizens and their representatives—have worked so steadfastly toward justice and equity?

On the day I was finishing the rough draft of this article, March 13, I hosted the fifth heartwarming gathering at my home. Before we called the evening to a close, we gathered our attention for a rain meditation. The catastrophic lack of snow in our hometown of Taos, New Mexico, meant we were all concerned about the land and water, along with the plants and animals that depend on those systems. We closed our eyes, became quiet, and visualized the clouds coming from the Southwest. Then we listened for the thunder and imagined the clouds darkening and gathering. Opening our eyes a few minutes later, one person said, "Aho."

Sitting together that night with our hearts open in sincerity, we renewed the core value of the Constitution as We the People acting in unison.

After carrying our cups to the kitchen and pulling on coats and gloves, we walked outside together into the relatively mild night. We were just in time to see the full moon rising—still orange and almost blossoming. As we stood absorbing the beauty, the clouds started to gather, and very soon they almost obscured the moon—except for its light, which illuminated the outlines of the clouds. Before the last person drove away, the moon was entirely concealed behind dark clouds. In the middle of the night, the wind was wild—even scary. But when I awoke in the morning, it was to snow on the ground.

Love, intention, and care all seemed to have played a part in bringing the moisture to Taos. And snow was even better than rain.

Endnotes

[1] For more on Prigogine's ideas, see *Order Out of Chaos: Man's New Dialogue with Nature*, coauthored with Isabelle Stengers, published first in French (1978), and later in English (1984).

[2] A good portion of the content about Gouverneur Morris was inspired by an interview with three Morris scholars on "We the People," a podcast. Constitutional law scholar Jeffrey Rosen interviewed the three (Melanie Miller, William Treanor, and Dennis Rasmussen) for an episode titled "The Life and Constitutional Legacy of Gouverneur Morris." Their books are listed below. https://constitutioncenter.org/news-debate/podcasts/the-life-and-constitutional-legacy-of-gouverneur-morris, accessed Jan. 6, 2025.

For further reading on Gouverneur Morris, see the books and articles by authors interviewed on the podcast:

Miller, Melanie Randolph, ed. (2018). *The Gouverneur Morris Papers: Diaries Project.* University of Virginia Press. She also authored two books on Morris: *Envoy to the Terror: Gouverneur Morris and the French Revolution* and *An Incautious Man: The Life of Gouverneur Morris.*

Rasmussen, Dennis C. (2023). *The Constitution's Penman: Gouverneur Morris and the Creation of America's Basic Charter,* University of Kansas.

Treanor, W. (2023). "Gouverneur Morris and the drafting of the federalist constitution," Georgetown Journal of Law and Public Policy, Winter 2023.

[3] Retrieved from the Library of Congress website: https://www.loc.gov/resource/bdsdcc.c01a2?st=grid on Jan. 10, 2025.

References

Arendt, H. (1976). *The Origins of Totalitarianism,* Mariner Books, p. 306.

Mitchell, S. (1992). *Tao te Ching.* Harper Perennial, p. 15.

We the People podcast: "The Life and Constitutional Legacy of Gouverneur Morris," with host Jeffrey Rosen and guests Melanie Miller, William Treanor, and Dennis Rasmussen.

Dreams of the US President 2024

Kelly Bulkeley and Jennifer Marie Lane

T he domain of meaning in dreaming extends beyond the personal sphere of individual daily concerns to include social experiences relating to collective concerns. Although still a controversial claim, there is mounting evidence in favor of this as a basic principle of dream phenomenology. A communal dimension of dream significance appears in classic religious texts, such as Pharaoh's dreams of coming famine in the Bible's book of Genesis and Muhammad's pre-battle dreams in the Qu'ran. The theme of dreams as a collective source of insight and guidance can be found in anthropological studies of cultural groups from virtually every part of the world, from Siberia to the Amazon, from Iceland to Hawaii, from Egypt to the Great Lakes (Von Grunebaum and Callois, 1966; Tedlock 1988; Mittermaier 2003; Mageo and Sheriff 2022). Instances abound in contemporary Western societies, too, in the form of dreams relating to collective events like firestorms, wars, terrorist attacks, the pandemic, and, less disastrously, films, celebrities, sports, and holidays (Siegel 1993, Bulkeley and Kahan

2008). Carl Jung had a prophetic dream of World War I; Freud dreamed about a reactionary Austrian politician. Charlotte Beradt's remarkable book *The Third Reich of Dreams* details the experience of dreaming in conditions of political oppression (Beradt 1966). Martin Luther King, Jr., was reassured by a 'midnight "kitchen vision" to continue his fight for

dimensions of dreaming (e.g., Bulkeley 2008). This research has continued and expanded since then, resulting most recently in the biggest project to date, *2020 Dreams* (Gutman and Bulkeley 2023), an all-digital, multi-authored work of scholarship that analyzes more than two thousand dream reports gathered during the year 2020 by correlating

> The domain of meaning in dreaming extends beyond the personal sphere of individual daily concerns to include social experiences relating to collective concerns.

social justice (Davis 2009). The point, which only seems strange from an individualistic Western perspective, is that whatever else we say about the nature of dreaming, we have good evidence showing it is deeply interwoven into the social fabric of our collective lives together.

In this context, one of the co-authors (KB) began a line of research in 1992 focused on dreams relating to US Presidential elections, pursuing the hypothesis that the attention and emotional energy aroused by the election campaigns would have a tangible impact on people's dreaming, which would highlight the bigger point about the collective

patterns in the dreams with patterns in the daily news as reported by the Associated Press. Over the course of these three decades of research, several recurrent themes have emerged that will influence our approach and analysis in this article. First is that contemporary Americans do indeed dream about politics and politicians, especially about Presidents and presidential candidates. Sometimes these dreams are very positive, sometimes very negative, and sometimes they are surprisingly personal and even intimate. This article presents several reports of this kind.

Previous findings have prompted a

Kelly Bulkeley is a dream researcher, author, and director of the Sleep and Dream Database. **Jennifer Marie Lane** is a dream researcher, author, and chiropractor.

more specific hypothesis that people's dreams of a politician represent a measure of that politician's charisma, as the term is used by the sociologist Max Weber (Gerth and Mills 1946). For Weber, charismatic political authority is opposed to the traditional practices of patriarchal authority and the rational systems of bureaucratic authority. In times of distress, "natural leaders" emerge whose power derives not from reason or tradition but from their special gifts of body and spirit and their charismatic capacity to elicit trust, enthusiasm, and devotion in their followers. To the extent this concept applies to the oneiric realm, we can measure a politician's charisma by the frequency of their appearance in people's dreams and the relational quality of their presence in those dreams. Earlier studies of the high frequencies and intimate/spiritual qualities of people's dreams about Bill Clinton in 1992 and 1996 and Barack Obama in 2008 and 2012 led to a predictive notion: *The candidate about whom people dream the most is the one most likely to win the given election.* As this article will show, dreams during the election of 2024 supports that predictive notion, albeit in a different ideological register from the earlier studies.

Sources and Methods

The present study draws upon a survey conducted on behalf of the Sleep and Dream Database by YouGov, a professional opinion research company. The sample size was 3,055 American adults (age 18 or older) (1,453 male, 1,602 female). Fieldwork was undertaken between 23rd - 26th September, 2024. The survey was conducted using an online interview administered to members of the YouGov panel of individuals who have agreed to take part in surveys. Emails were sent to panelists selected at random from the base sample. The e-mail invited them to take part in a survey and provided a generic survey link. Once a panel member clicked on the link they were sent to the survey that they were most required for, according to the sample definition and quotas. (The sample definition could be "US adult population" or a subset such as "US adult females"). Invitations to surveys don't expire and respondents can be sent

to any available survey. The responding sample is weighted to the profile of the sample definition to provide a representative reporting sample. The profile is normally derived from census data or, if not available from the census, from industry accepted data. YouGov make every effort to provide representative information. All results are based on a sample and are therefore subject to statistical errors normally associated with sample-based information.

This survey, conducted approximately six weeks before the US Presidential Election, asked participants two questions specifically related to the election: one, which Presidential candidate do you support, and two, have you experienced a dream relating to the election. If the

participants answered yes to the dream question, they were asked to describe the dream in as much detail as they felt comfortable.

There are many limits to this kind of empirical research. Surveys offer no interaction with the dreamers, and thus no opportunity for follow-up questions and collaborative interpretation. We only have access to their self-reports and their other survey answers. Furthermore, people can be reluctant to share private details in an impersonal research context, and even when they try to be forthcoming, people sometimes edit or revise their dreams to appear more pleasing to the questioner. This can limit how far we generalize from the dream reports we do gather, encouraging us always to recognize these dreams are but a fraction of the totality of collective dreaming at a given moment in time.

Taking these limits into account, the great benefit for dream research of a demographic survey methodology is the opportunity to hear dreams from a wide variety of people in society as a whole. Experience has shown that

many forms of dream research—e.g., psychotherapy sessions, college student experiments, laboratory studies, open calls for dreams—tend to over-sample some groups and under-sample other groups. Of relevance for this article, typical dream research methods often include higher proportions of women and/or political liberals and lower proportions of men and/or political conservatives. The reasons for that imbalance are complex and interesting, but beyond the scope of this paper to discuss. Suffice it to say that a primary justification for using a demographic survey methodology, despite its limitations, is that it helps us cast a wider and more systematic net to gather new information about how dreaming reflects our social and political

Previous findings have prompted a more specific hypothesis that people's dreams of a politician represent a measure of that politician's charisma, as the term is used by the sociologist Max Weber.

lives. The results will be best understood as providing a complementary empirical resource for other methods of inquiry, all working together towards a greater appreciation of dreaming as a wellspring of collective insight and guidance.

Results

A total of 220 participants provided a response to the dream report question. After carefully reading and re-reading the reports, the co-authors sorted the reports from Trump and Harris supporters (setting aside the 11 reports from supporters of third-party candidates) into seven categories: General dreams about the election, Trump victory, Harris victory, Trump nightmare, Harris nightmare, Civil disorder, and Encounter with a Politician. Below are samples of reports from each category. An eighth category is included for the small number of invalid responses. The entire collection of dreams is available upon request for further study in the Sleep and Dream Database (SDDb). All quotes below are the complete unedited responses from the participants. Only a final period has been added to the end of a report when needed. After each report, the participant's identification number for this survey is included, along with a "T" if the person indicated they are a Trump supporter and an "H" for a self-identified Harris supporter.

General dreams about the election.

Reports in this category (a total of 30) include references to the experience of voting, campaigning, debates, polls, and generic presidential candidates. Several of these dreams associate the election with positive social interactions. Many more Harris supporters (26) than Trump supporters (4) reported dreams of this type.

"that i went to vote and saw the candidates." (1217, H)

"I had a dream about elections. There were people going to vote and they were happy." (1821, H)

"I went to the polls and met a lot of my old friends, and we had a great chat." (116, H)

"Dreamed about standing in line waiting to vote and seeing random people I know." (210, H)

Other reports in this category are less favorably disposed toward the process.

"I fell into a hole while going to the elections." (1903, T)

"I dreamed that about the debate cause that's all they talk about on social media." (1935, H)

Trump victory.

Most of these dreams (32 in total) are reported in brief, straightforward fashion.

"Donald Trump wins the election." (1580, T)

"Trump won." (2310, T)

"Trump won.. thank god." (698, T)

"Kamala loses by a landslide." (1605, T)

A few of the dreams in this category express social and emotional positivity.

"Trump D. Was triumphant and we were all jubilating with our family. And i woke up." (2543, T)

"I was in a crowd in NYC like Times Square. Everyone was there for Trump. He had won but I woke up before he came. I've never been to Times Square." (2602, T)

Harris victory.

The same number of dreams in this survey collection (32) anticipated a Harris victory, many in similarly brief, straightforward terms.

"Kamla Harris wins." (96, H)

"I dreamt that Kamala won." (1005, H)

"I dreamed that it was a landslide victory for kamala Harris." (2042, H)

And several of these dreams also express social and emotional positivity.

"Kamala Harris becomes the first Black woman to win the election. People nationwide celebrate her victory." (3085, H)

"I dreamed that we were in DC for the inauguration of Harris- we will be there if she wins- so maybe that's why I dreamt about it." (2455, H)

Trump nightmare.

These reports (23 in total) do not anticipate a Trump victory from a supporter's perspective; on the contrary, they express a host of negative emotions in relation to his winning the election, all from Harris supporters.

"I've had nightmares where Trump wins. And I feel terrible and afraid." (720, H)

"Anxiety dream about the horrific result if trump gets back into office. I woke up having a panic attack and had a migraine all day." (921, H)

"Trump was elected and I woke up in a panicked sweat. It was a nightmare." (982, H)

"Nightmares, really, not dreams. I experience a wave of fear related to Trump being elected, and then a variety of storylines wherein he has me arrested, imprisoned or deported for my issue advocacy or political activism." (2447, H)

A subset of four dreams specifically mention Margaret Atwood's dystopian novel *The Handmaid's Tale* as an anticipated nightmare consequence of his victory.

"Trump won and a real life handmaid's tale started." (98, H)

"Trump winning and handsmaids tale begins." (1003, H)

"I have agonized and stressed over this election. Usually my dreams relate to me losing my

rights and living in a world similar to a combination of a handmaiden's tale and ww2." (1298, H)*

"I had a nightmare where everything was a mash-up of 1950s stepford wives and Handmaid's Tale Gilead under a Trump administration." (2770, H)

Harris nightmare.

There were fewer Harris nightmares reported in this survey (13 in total) compared to Trump nightmares. The nightmares about Harris, all from Trump supporters, also express fear for personal and collective safety, although they do not offer as many emotional details or recurrent themes.

"It was more of a nightmare. The dream was waking up on November 6th and Kamala Harris was the winner of the election." (2817, T)

"The fear of Harris taking over our wonderful country!" (540, T)

"Dream of Kamala winning election and the disaster befalling this country should that happen." (756, T)

"Trump lost elections and Harris won and completely destroyed our democracy and caused total chaos!" (3035, T)

"I dreamed that Harris won and God was totally against it that he came back to save the world but woke up before anything was done." (872, T)

"The democrats won, and I became an expat in Costa Rica. Sold everything I own here, and took myself and my dogs far FAR away." (190, T)

Civil disorder.

The dreams in this category (29 in total) involve various kinds of public conflict and violence--riots, assassinations, civil war, disrupting the elections, or fighting over the results.

"Trump loses and the riots start then Harris is the winner and the riots start." (274, H)

"There was a lot of blood shed people running away from soldiers." (653, T)

"I saw in my dream where civil war broke out in America." (1123, T)

"Chaos." (1857, T)

"I saw Kamala Harris dressed in dark tan/brown pants suit. She was making a speech that I couldn't make out. Then I saw Her leading Trump in the polls. Then I saw Trump giving a speech, saying. "STOP THE VOTE" and I saw people showing up to the polls armed. I had this dream about a week before Biden left the race." (1007, H)

"I've had nightmares of another January 6th, since I was there working and was trapped alone for 8+ hours." (2227, H)

Several of the reports in this survey refer to the assassination attempts against then-candidate Trump on July 13 and on September 15, the latter just eight days before the survey's launch. If references to Trump dying before the election are included, eight of the dreams have this particular theme. Here are two instances.

"Crazy as it might sound, I once dreamt about the assassination on Trump as a facade to shoot up his odds and he influencially won the election." (1159, H)

"Illegal immigrants storming in a debate in an attempt to assassinate Trump." (3164, T)

Encounter with a Politician.

These dreams (44 in total) are less abstract than the others. The dreamer doesn't just think about a politician, but has a personal encounter with them, which in the dream state can feel experientially real. The scenarios of this type of dream include talking with a politician, exchanging gifts, sharing a meal, being together at a party or at the dreamer's home. Also included here are reports in which the dreamer dreams of becoming President themselves. Here are several instances of Trump encounters:

"I dreamed that I got to meet Donald Trump and he gave me a MAGA hat."(196, T)

"Trump was a guest at an event I attended. We interacted somewhat." (210, H)

"I dreamed we met President Trump." (466, T)

"I have dreamed of Pres Trump in my parents' home, and it was summertime and hot. Yet he was dressed in his suit and tie. And I wondered that he would be so hot

all dressed up." (1354, T)

"I have had dreams in which Donald Trump appears. I don't remember other details." (2294, H)

"I met Donald Trump, and was repelled and fascinated. He wasn't as charismatic as I expected, just soft spoken, old and weak." (2476, H)

"A friend of mine who passed away was walking arm and arm with trump. I said to her get him away from me. She chuckled and literally skipped off with him." (2705, H)

"Memory has faded but several bad dreams involving Donald Trump." (2073, H)

Here are several instances of Harris encounters:

"I dreamed Kamala Harris had something on her face, she was obscured by a shadow covering what she had done. Her hands were up like she was shrugging her shoulders. The dream was in color. Her suit was dark, her shirt was cream colored, her hair was messy because something caused it to be messy. There were drops of rain obscuring my vision, but I could see it was her." (589, T)

"dreaming that I was next to Harris, who had just been appointed president, and we were having coffee at Starbucks." (1115, H)

"I don't remember much, but it involved Kamala Harris. She was at some kind of small event that I attended. There were maybe 50 people there and she addressed the group." (1642, H)

"I dreamed about Kamala Harris and Tim Walz. It was a pleasant dream, and they were at some kind of event I was at, just walking around and talking to people there." (1693, H)

"Kamala Harris was arguing with some guy while I was fishing on a dock and then Tim Walz drunkenly stumbled up behind her to admonish this guy and got so flustered that he fell into the water." (2337, H)

The following three reports describe dream experiences of especially intense political content.

"I was driving down as rural road and the further I got the deeper the woods got and the bigger the Trump signs (for president) got and they were just engulfing me The roads were narrowing and then what I'd call floodgates opened up then what I'd basically describe as Nazi zombies were coming out of all these trailer like structures. It woke me up. It wasn't a dream. It was a nightmare and it just freaked me out. Earlier in the week I had actually gone on a drive through a couple rural Maine towns with a bunch of trump/vance signs It did makee feel a bit uncomfortable at the time. Apparently my subconscious took it a lot harder!" (115, H)

"I had a dream related to the 2024 US election just last week. In my dream, I was attending a rally for Donald Trump, and I was impressed by his passionate speech. However, the scene suddenly shifted to a debate between Trump and Kamala Harris, where they were discussing economic policies. It was vivid and felt so real." (1492, T)

"I had a dream that is based in reality that I got back in touch with a friend who is now a Trump supporter. In the dream this friend now hates me. This does happen often to dreams that are semi based in reality, or that have a likelihood of what could happen. As well in my dreams that are based in reality I somehow die at the end of every dream." (1014, H)

Looking at the whole set of 220 dream responses, Donald Trump is mentioned or appears in 97 of them. Kamala Harris appears in 61. Joe Biden and Tim Walz appear in 4 reports each, J.D. Vance in 3, and the following figures appear once each: Hillary Clinton, Robert F. Kennedy, Jr., Elon Musk, Tom Hanks, Drake, Nicolas Maduro, Charlie Kirk, and Vivek Ramaswamy.

Discussion

Keeping the previously stated limits in mind, the results of this survey sheds new light on several important points in the study of the interactions between dreaming, politics, and culture. First and most fundamentally, these results provide further evidence that at least some people do dream about politics and electoral campaigns. This supports the idea that dream content, in addition to purely personal concerns, also includes references to issues and events of collective concern. Second, the results illustrate the various ways in which political themes enter the contents of dreaming. Both major party candidates appear in the dreams here, reported by supporters of both candidates, in both very positive and very negative emotional terms. Rather than some kind of narrow partisan phenomenon, politically-themed dreaming seems to be distributed broadly across the ideological spectrum.

A third finding to highlight here concerns the relative numbers of dream references to the two major party can-

those of dreams about Obama). These dream patterns may be coincidental with electoral results, of course, but they are also consistent with the notion that what connects a politician's dream appearances and electoral success is the quality of charisma. In Max Weber's account, charisma is a disruptive form of political authority that ignores bureaucratic rationality and traditional practices in favor of leadership by specially blessed, divinely-sanctioned figures whose power draws upon the intense devotion of their followers. These attributes of charismatic leadership—the strong emotionality, spiritual enthusiasm, transformative hope, and relational bonding—make it fertile territory for dreaming, much more so than conventional types of political authority. This is not necessarily good or bad; as Weber himself says, "the

Conclusion.

The results of this study leave many important questions unanswered about the meaning and long-term significance of the 2024 American Presidential election. But the findings here may have value in raising new questions that only come into view once we recognize the significance of these political themes in people's dreaming. For instance, how long does political charisma last? Do ongoing patterns of dream content reflect both the waxing and the waning of people's charismatic attachment to a certain politician? To what extent may we envision a political leader, movement, or party intentionally trying to stimulate people's dreaming engagement and responsiveness? If politicians are already doing this at some unconscious level, what more could they do if they made a more conscious, focused effort to inspire their followers' dreams? Could this become a harmful process if the goal became nothing more than trying to arouse nightmares about one's opponents?

Another set of questions raised by this study concerns the possibility of the systematic analysis of dream content enabling us to track the early development of charismatic leadership and its emergence in the public sphere. We might want to try identifying individuals about whom other people are dreaming at an unusually high frequency and consider the possibility that such dreams indicate a potential for charismatic leadership in those individuals. This will be a challenge for dream researchers, who will need to move beyond the general demographics of the present study to explore in more detail the social psychology of smaller groups where particular figures may be the subject of intense and frequent dreaming among other group members. But if the insights can be extended to this level of analysis, we may find that in people's dreams of today we can witness the emergence of the future leaders of tomorrow.

> Rather than some kind of narrow partisan phenomenon, politically-themed dreaming seems to be distributed broadly across the ideological spectrum.

didates. Reading through the entire collection of 220 responses, we find 97 references to Trump and 61 references to Harris. This is a large difference, and as noted in the Introduction, previous studies have suggested that being the candidate more people dream about correlates with being the candidate more people vote for. This was most vividly true with Bill Clinton, about whom many more people dreamed than about his opponents George W. Bush and Ross Perot in 1992 (although Perot had a brief spike of dream appearances) and Bob Dole in 1996, and with Barack Obama, who had much higher frequencies of people dreaming about him than his opponents John McCain in 2008 and Mitt Romney in 2012 (although during the 2008 Democratic primaries, the frequencies of dreams about Hillary Clinton rivaled

concept of 'charisma' is here used in a completely 'value-neutral' sense" (Gerth and Mills 1946, 245). In this light, what is striking about the present survey is that it demonstrates an ideological flexibility in the interactions of dreaming and charismatic leadership. Previously, these dynamics of dreaming, charisma, and electoral success were most easily observed among the supporters of left-of-center Democrats like Bill and Hillary Clinton and Barack Obama, with less evidence of such dream phenomena among the supporters of right-of-center Republican politicians. However, the results of the 2024 election, both electorally and oneirically, indicate that a similar, charismatically inflected pattern of disparate dream references between two candidates can work to the favor of the right as well as the left.

References

Beradt, C. (1966). *The Third Reich of Dreams.* Adriane Gottwald, trans. Chicago: Quadrangle Books.

Bulkeley, K. (2008). *American Dreamers: What Dreams Tell Us about the Political Psychology of Conservatives, Liberals, and Everyone Else.* Boston: Beacon Press.

Bulkeley, K., & Tracey L. K. (2008). "The Impact of September 11 on Dreaming." *Consciousness and Cognition* 17:1248-1256.

Davis, P. M. (2009). "Auditory Revelations in Dreaming," in Kelly Bulkeley, Kate Adams, & Patricia M. Davis (Eds.), *Dreaming in Christianity and Islam: Culture, Conflict, and Creativity.* New Brunswick: Rutgers University Press.

Gerth, H.H. & Wright Mills, C. (Eds. & Trans.) (1946). *From Max Weber: Essays in Sociology.* New York: Oxford University Press.

Gutman, M., & Bulkeley K. (2023). *2020 Dreams.* Stanford: Stanford University Press.

Heijnen, A. (2003). *The Social Life of Dreams: A Thousand Years of Negotiated Meanings in Iceland.* Zurich: Lit Verlag.

Mageo, J., & Sheriff, R. (Eds.) (2022). *New Directions in the Anthropology of Dreaming.* New York: Palgrave Macmillan.

Mittermaier, A. (2010). *Dreams That Matter: Egyptian Landscapes of the Imagination.* Berkeley: University of California Press, .

Siegel, A. (1993). "Dreams of Firestorm Survivors," in D. Barrett (Ed.), *Trauma and Dreams.* Cambridge: Harvard University Press.

Tedlock, B. (Ed.) (1989). *Dreaming: Anthropological and Psychological Interpretations.* New York: Oxford University Press.

Von Grunebaum, G.E., & Callois, R. (Eds.) (1966). *The Dream and Human Societies.* Berkeley: University of California Press.

A Small Dust of Life
by Chun Yu

What a miracle it is
to have fallen to this blue planet
as a small dust of life
to be born through
my beautiful mother
on your bountiful land
and open my eyes
to the unprecedented
creation and revolution
humankind has undertaken?

Yet, in the glory of your mountains
the splendor of your waters
our ultimate ego unfolds
in final pursuit of desires.

In a mere short century
you endured us in silence
while our desperate needs
driven by an unfathomable force
depletes you like a mother suckling
her last young, who must take all
    they can
for their prodigal destiny.

Day and night, we slave over
what will take us away from you
so we can go up to the sky
the starlit playground
forever fantasized for.

When we finally manage to
pierce into Earth and ascend into
    Space
we realize, as if waking up from
    a dream
that we will have no choice but
to find new grounds to survive on.

Coming to Earth in this life
I am in boundless love and grief –

I don't want to drift back
into the sky, the great void
so unbearably far and cold.
I only want to morph back
into the small dust of life on Earth
and mingle like ash
with your warm soil

with the billion beings
that cannot leave.

Together, we will wait
in hope, to return to
the glory of your flowers
the splendor of your grass.

Author's Note: The last two lines are in honor of William Wordsmith and his poem Ode: Intimations of Immortality from Recollections of Early Childhood:

*"Though nothing can bring back
    the hour
Of splendour in the grass, of
    glory in the flower,
We will grieve not, rather find
Strength in what remains
    behind…"*

Walking Home in Silence

John Heckel

With Poetry from American Silos

Michael Bickford

How could what happened have happened?

I was born in Germany immediately after World War II. I spent much of my early childhood asking questions. How could you have let this happen? Didn't you know what was going on? Questions that received very few acceptable answers. Our family immigrated to the United States in 1954.

Now I was asked questions to which I could give very few acceptable answers. How could your parents have let that happen? Didn't they know what was

John Heckel is a retired professor of theatre and film at Humboldt State University. John has directed both film and theatre, educationally and professionally. He has been fortunate enough to have lived, taught and directed in multiple foreign countries. After serving as his mother's primary care-giver until her death at the age of 95, John went back to school to receive a Ph.D. in psychology. He currently advocates for seniors, directs the occasional play, does gender and couples therapy consulting, and writes articles and a monthly column on the difficulties of aging.

Michael Bickford was born in Los Angeles, and escaped north. After an extensive street education, he received a teaching credential from San Francisco State University. He lives on California's Redwood Coast, where he writes poetry and fiction with the Lost Coast Writers Community, Inc, of which he is a founding member. His dual-language chapbook, Mrs. Silva Walks to the Azores (with Portuguese translation by 2023 National Book Award winner Bruna Dantas Lobato) is a recent release from Finishing Line Press.

going on?

It was not until my 21st birthday (1967) that I found out, through a confessional conversation with my mother, that my father had been a member of The Young Communist League of Germany. As a member, his activities included

> Bring down the silos
> that separate us
> burst excluding bubbles
> crush the cones of silence
> open up the echo chambers of
> our politics.
>
> I have no illusion of seeing this
> in my lifetime.
> These structures took too long to
> build,
> and are built of too costly a
> material:
> the very human lives,
> filled with human fault and folly,
> that have brought us to this
> painful polarization.

distributing party newspapers, painting anti-Nazi graffiti-slogans, posting anti-Nazi posters and agitprop (political propaganda) theatre. As a result of his activities, he was arrested and sent to Kemna Concentration Camp in 1933, a mere 30 miles from his hometown. Pris-

oners and guards came from the same neighborhoods. They knew each other. When Hitler closed the camp on January 19, 1934, guards and prisoners walked back home to the same neighborhoods. Two grotesquely different world views were walking home in silence, neither questioning the other until many decades later.

It seems questioning extreme moments of polarization is coded into my DNA.

An Attempt at Understanding Polarization

Through the modern wonder of social media, I left my confirmation-bias-bubble and learned, in the fall of 2020, of the countless folks I went to high school with who were now avid and open Trump supporters. So, I reached out, in an attempt to understand how it was that we had drifted so far apart, with the proposition that we discuss our differences, with particular emphasis on events in our lives that had led us to those differing world views.

My Post of September 10, 2020:

I went to high school from 1960 to 1964. A wonderful and remarkable aspect of social media is the ability to stay connected with friends and colleagues from long ago. I have around twenty-five or so friends from those high school days, of those some 40% have come out adamantly and publicly for Trump. These are all people who went to a university, are all, if not well off, financially comfortable.

I openly admit I have gone through our Maine West 1964 yearbook, looking at your faces. Yes, Ruth, Tom, Steve, Kieth, Lou and others, you know who you are. I did, I looked you up, re-read about the activities we shared, the plays and V-shows we did together. I did all this in a desperate attempt to understand where our thoughts, insights and views became so polarized.

Help me understand. Were we that different back then and we simply didn't know? If not, what was the turning/tipping point?

I long to understand. I do not want to change your mind. I know nothing I can say will do that. I invite your opinion, not about Trump, but about how we became so polarized.

I invite you to a dialogue between people who came of age in the early sixties, in the suburbs of Chicago, who went to football games together, who built homecoming floats together, whose heart skipped a beat when Maureen was chosen homecoming queen....and all those other coming of age initiations.... now grown into elders who cannot speak to each other with civility when it comes to Trump... What happened?

To suggest my invitation was a failure would be an understatement. My attempt at creating a dialogue triggered six months of sarcasm, vitriol and anger. I ignorantly expected a group of seventy-plus-year-olds to be able to do something our American-White-Patriarchal culture not only does not encourage but actively discourages: to engage across our differences.

I cite two examples as being indicative of the offensive and divisive language, attitude, and emotion as well as group stereotyping my request engendered—

Posted September 11, 2020

"I believe they are just unedu-cated and untrained in empathy for anyone who is not just like them (aka white, Christian, selfish.) BTW, I would be amazed if you get any responses—in my experience, none of them will answer questions like yours—they are only comfort-able in packs."

From the other side—
Posted September 12, 2020

"Of course, you are aware that the majority of abortions are of black babies and the Dems are ok with KILLING a baby AFTER it is born. Yes. There are many of us. We will not be bullied by the Dems who think they are the elites and we better listen.....or else.

Nice talking to you, John!!!

My neighbor raised around the block from me
in a similar silo—now blood red:
FUCK YOUR FEELINGS plastered his walls
like a rural ad for tractors on a barn;
Let's Go Brandon meaning
Fuck You Biden;
Stars & Stripes in black & blue
a Thin Blue Line,
of corporate troops in a race war;

I thought I could change my neighbor's mind if I spoke
Truth to Power, but he had none;
that if I said the right words he'd change his mind—
and we could be as close as neighbors should—
but I feared his guns, and said nothing.

My initial attempt at opening a dialogue for understanding felt like a complete failure.

I would discover several years later the necessary elements for any real understanding, active listening, and speaking with intention.

A More Thought-out Attempt at Understanding Polarization

I write a monthly column on aging for a Northern California newspaper and have been doing so since 1995. I often find ways to process personal issues through writing that column, and I did so with the despair I felt with that first disastrous attempt at dialogue.

Attempts at self-discovery do not always move in straight and direct lines. They sometimes travel in mysterious and circuitous routes. My post on social media, the resulting vitriol, and my column were read by a former under-graduate colleague of mine in Portland, Oregon, Dick Dezeeuw. He and I had attended Drake University together in the mid 60's and had been members of the same fraternity. He sent me an email.

Posted August 21, 2021:

John- You may not remember me, but I was a Pike at Drake a year or so behind you. I was inspired by your column and postings last year about reaching out to old friends and acquaintances to discuss how you had simi-lar early lives but now have such different world views. Want to try again?

I responded with an enthusi-astic affirmation.

We soon recruited another fraternity brother, Rick Sline, living in Florida, and the three of us set off on a three-month journey to find a structure for dialoguing around what divides us and form a working zoom group that would agree to follow and experiment with that structure.

First meeting November 11, 2021

We quickly agreed the most diffi-cult task in our experiment would be forming and then facilitating a group to share polarizing world views. Since I had almost no contact with any of the proposed participants, I relied on the judgement of my two colleagues. They did have history with the potential participants and based on that history we invited forty fraternity brothers to participate. Twelve accepted immediately, four declined and the rest did not respond to our emailed invitations. Our assessment was that our group of twelve provided the diversity of world views needed to make our experiment work.

The initial meeting of the group focused on a basic understanding of Zoom protocols, personal histories and updates on what everyone had been doing since graduating from Drake University fifty some years ago, and an explanation of the structured dialogues we intended to follow. Our initial assessment about diversity of world views proved mostly correct. After three men dropped out before the first meeting, we were nine, of which five were liberal leaning participants, and four adamant Trump supporters. Everyone agreed to meet for 90 minutes every two weeks.

Facilitators agreed to create and send out via email dialogue topics at least three days before meeting. As facilitators we also took on the responsibility of creating and then enforcing a structure that we believed had a chance of successfully holding and containing the emotions triggered by our planned dialogues.

Meeting Structure and Hopes for that Structure

As facilitators we formulated the following meeting structure:

Facilitator's Introduction

Re-Introduction of meeting topic as previously sent via email, reminder of structure and explanation or cause of anyone missing.

First Round:

Participants each have three minutes of uninterrupted speaking time to share their view regarding the stated topic. The hope is that providing participants with no cross-talking time, to express their views, will develop a willingness to share and create a meaningful level of vulnerability. Facilitators will choose first person to speak who will then choose the next speaker. A silent pause of 15 seconds between each speaker, during which time participants are encouraged to write down clarifying questions for round three. No cross-talking.

Facilitator Remarks:

Second round is re-introduced, restating the self-reflective process of finding events in our earlier years that shaped or influenced the stated world views of round one.

Second Round:

Participants each have three minutes of uninterrupted speaking time to share their thoughts on what life experiences have shaped or influenced their views as expressed in round one. The hope is that establishing a relationship between worldviews (first round) and actual lived experiences (second round) invites empathy and understanding. Facilitators will choose first person to speak and then that person will choose the next participant. A silent pause of 15 seconds between speakers, during which time participants are encouraged to write down clarifying questions for round three. No cross talk.

Facilitator Remarks:

Third round is introduced with the guideline of asking questions for clarification and not for argumentation or disagreement. Participants are reminded that the inflection pattern and tone of their questions are as important as the question's word choice. The hope is that stressing "questions for clarification" will invite curious and information-seeking questions rather than reactive ones.

Third Round:

Depending on time considerations, the Third Round is 15 or so minutes of clarifying questions.

Facilitator Remarks:

Final wrap and a reminder of our next scheduled meeting.

Shared Facilitator Responsibility:

Responsibility for remarks and enforcement of the structure is always shared equally among facilitators. Our hope is that in each session we model individual voices within a supportive collective.

Silos as keeps, redoubts, watchtowers, hoards;
Fort Apache at the edge of conquest
of peoples, nations, homelands,
sovereignty ripped from bodies
politic   water   earth,
by force of inferior moral arms
to terrorize, dehumanize, to kill
the people here, in this untitled land.
Rematriate   Rematriate   Rematriate and free us all.

Language Choices that Encourage Understanding

From the very start we agreed as facilitators we would also participate in each meeting's dialogue. We also agreed that our language choices would be critical to the potential success of our project and that as participants, we have an important role in modeling those language choices. Adopting neutral and inviting language choices that encourage understanding is critical for our group cohesiveness and ultimate success. *Clarifying questions* was a particular fortuitous choice and *dialogue* was another.

The consistent use of the word *dialogue* to describe our process soon had a profound effect on our participants and their use of language. We are interested in language that nurtures understanding. We shared with the participants the basis for its use in the spirit of David Bohm, Donald Factor and Peter Garrett (1991) from *Dialogue--A Proposal*:

Dialogue, as we are choosing to use the word, is a way of exploring the roots of the many crises that face humanity today. It enables inquiry into, and understanding of, the sorts of processes that fragment and interfere with real communication between individuals, nations and even different parts of the same organization. In our modern culture men and women are able to interact with one another in many ways: they can sing, dance or play together with little difficulty, but their ability to talk together about subjects that matter deeply to them seems invariably to lead to dispute, division and often to violence (david-bohm.net).

On a personal note, the transformative power of genuine dialogue has been part of my consciousness since pursuing a PhD in psychology. It was also an essential aspect of my dissertation on transgressive gender performances. My belief in the self-reflective and transformative power of dialogue is rooted in my work in both theatre and psychology.

Of all the reminders that we as facilitators suggested to individual participants, "Please, use language that encourages understanding", was by far the most frequent. All too often participants' language choices and inflection patterns hindered understanding. I offer more thoughts on language choices in the following section on learnings.

Participants

The 1960's was a decade of profound transition and transformation. Our participants experienced those transitions, and many found them transformative. From the early to mid-sixties, our group collectively experienced it all: fraternity parties, letterman jackets, and basketball games—and then in the late sixties and early seventies draft card burning, long hair war protests, along with those who enlisted and served with commitment.

Half our group served in the military and half demonstrated and protested the war.

We are all straight white men with at least one university degree. Some comment on this seems appropriate. We've had several intense dialogues addressing the early racist and homophobic nature of all-white-straight fraternities and the role we played in that culture. Not an easy dialogue to be sure, but necessary, given the nature and history of our group. They seemed, to me, to have been productive.

Participants in our group include a retired pharmacist, a nearly retired attorney who argued in front of the Supreme Court, two PhDs and several retired

To be woke at my dawn in land studded
with silos, a stubble of towers, red,
   black-n-white, blue, with interstitial green,
taller than trees—we burn those in the stoves—
in fruited alluvial plains we claim
to be ours from great-great-grandparents' sins,
      justifying   forgiving   forgetting
to look back to where I'm told we have come—
      as documented?   who can remember?
and see the gray silo I was born to,
      two-tone-faded   aged   not yet colorized,
on a ticky-tack suburban cul-de-sac,
and find myself here, in a blue silo,
full of kernels of truth and deep belief
      about belief, and wonder
            how far removed I am from red,
                  and how we got so far apart.

financial advisors. We are almost all retired and, in my estimate, comfortable financially. Most of us are grandfathers, some of us have been married three times, and some married to the same person for over fifty years.

Some of us find meaning in God through organized religion, others have found a more individualized path towards spirituality, still others reject religion and spirituality outright.

Every one of us has experienced moments of deep personal self-reflection and insight during the more than three years of our dialogues. All have expressed how much they value these meetings.

Topics

As of May 14, 2025 our dialogue group has met 73 times. We are now a group of eleven, in that we added two new members to the original group of nine in early January of 2025. We continue to tackle difficult polarizing topics. The previously outlined meeting structure has stayed pretty much the same. It has allowed us to share thoughts and feelings on very divisive topics.

A Random Sample of Topics:

December 2, 2021	Securing the integrity of the election process
December 9	White privilege and critical race theory
January 27, 2022	Immigration Policy
January 27	Police reform
February 10	The January 6 incident
February 24	First Trump presidency
March 10	Biden administration
March 24	Events in Ukraine
January 4, 2023	Reparations, slavery, and Native Americans
July 5	Recent Supreme Court decisions
September 6	Racism and sexist behavior in the fraternity system
October 4	Death and Dying— Death with dignity
October 18	War between Israel and Hamas
December 20	Political implications of a Trump victory
January 17, 2024	Mandatory public service
February 7	Important events of 2023 and hopes and fears for 2024
January 8, 2025	Shooting a CEO, violence and social change
January 22	The value of friendship in the aging process
February 12	Our values and

February 26   Patriotism

March 12   Evolving US relationship with Russia and the Ukraine

As the level of vulnerability has increased so have topics, and as the number of topics have increased so have our learnings. (See Let the Men Speak)

Learnings

The following learnings are the result of various inputs and observations. As facilitators, Rick, Dick and I would meet for fifteen or so minutes after each dialogue. During these post-session debriefs, we share our immediate, often, emotional reactions. We also always meet at least once in between group dialogues to further discussions and observations and plan the next polarizing topic. We also, twice, responded to each other's observations and learnings via prolonged written email exchanges.

On an annual basis, we also asked the group for feedback in the form of questionnaires, which were sent out during each year of our meetings. We continually asked for feedback regarding the structure of our meetings. Was the structure limiting, constrictive or in any way restricting their abilities to be vulnerable with their responses? Feedback was always supportive and grateful for our enforcement of that structure. Some of our learnings were influenced by that feedback. (See Let the Men Speak.)

Shared Commonality

A shared commonality was the reason the group was brought together. Group members shared a foundational commonality in attending the same university and membership in the same fraternity. The hope was that these commonalities created a preliminary basis for bonding while also lessening the tendency to otherize and polarize.

Sharing a basis in group commonality greatly facilitates discussions across individual differences. Some expressed and experienced commonality, be it membership in the same church, same service organization, same fraternity or having attended the same university. These common backgrounds and touchpoints grounded and allowed for a more authentic and vulnerable exploration of differences. The commonality carries weight and significance especially, in the first several dialogues and early stages of group development. The shared commonality must be experiential not simply theoretical, that is, rooted in readily identifiable shared experiences.

I grew up in a black-n-white silo.
Now I'm afraid of red silos; I've heard
the people in there are armed and alarmed,
    that they think I am
    what I really am:
        an atheist, socialist, humanist,
        scientist, feminist, drug addict, wimp;
that others in their blue silos
      are female, lesbian, liberal, queer,
    people of color, hedonists, vegan;
      that we hate them (I don't)
        and so they hate who we are
        and will kill us for being
        who we are   who I am.

Recognition of Triggering Life Events:

Many basic world views, such as the ones that so acutely divide our country, are set into motion or triggered by long ago life experiences. Worldviews expressed at 75 might easily have been formed by life events that occurred at

sciously hold that those world views are often derived from life experiences that took place long ago. Hearing another's direct experience also decreases the need to argue the speaker out of their held position.

Every dialogue has focused on both world views and life experiences that might lead to those world views. As our time together has increased, so has the significance the men place on life experiences. They seem slowly to be becoming more interested in examining those triggering life experiences. Sharing and hearing life experiences invites us into another person's reality, generating an empathetic bridge.

The Security of Commonality: During dialogues that explore emotionally packed differences, it is helpful to never drift far away from what the group holds in common. Taking time out to focus on that commonality, the shared experience of the university, church, fraternity or service club—tends to solidify the ground on which the dialogues on differences stand. In moments of discomfort or after moments of vulnerability, dialogue participants will, on their own initiative, if the structure allows, move to reconnecting on that shared commonality.

Group Structure as Ritual

If given the opportunity, the structure of the dialogues will take on many aspects of ritual. Effective ritual provides a safe container, a known and trusted holding space, for participants. Due to the emotional safety provided by a familiar structure, participants can take greater emotional risks in sharing and exploring polarizing subjects together.

Our participants gradually adopted and acted in ways to encourage each other to follow the agreed upon structure and find in that form significance and

> Hearing another's direct experience also decreases the need to argue the speaker out of their held position.

15. The patience and tolerance necessary to truly listen to and understand a subjectively objectionable expressed world view is increased if the listener can con-

meaning. Group members came to feel safety in the group structure, becoming not only observers but defenders of it.

An example--our group took the simple act of taking 15 seconds of silence between speakers and made it their own. Slowly over many sessions each participant began to verbalize taking those 15 seconds—" I am now going to wait 15 seconds!" or "I am going to take 15 seconds of silence." Each wording slightly different, but each took responsibility with the word "I." As of May 2025 every participant introduces their 15 seconds of silence, thereby each claiming ownership and commitment to the structure.

Language that Furthers Understanding:

The larger societal milieu in which our group is situated operates in a confirmational-bias-bubble that does not encourage the use of language for understanding across differences. Due to this societal conditioning, careless language choices can easily provoke argumentative responses and laughter. Language choices which engage sarcasm as a communication tool come easily but do little to further understanding. Choices that vulnerably encouraged understanding came much harder.

It may be that our identities, our egos, are more steeped in uses of language that encourage argumentative response rather than language that invites understanding. We may have become accustomed to people listening for response and are not comfortable with people listening for understanding.

Even though we, as facilitators, consistently expressed and defined the concept of clarifying questions, participants often fell back on argumentative or self-advancing questions. It is easy to embed commentary and opinion within the

phrasing of a question. After more than three years of work, section three of our dialogue structure—Clarifying Questions—still causes the group the greatest difficulty. Listening for understanding takes energy. It is an active form of listening. Speaking for understanding and choosing language that you believe fosters understanding also takes extra care and energy. It may very well be that the men in our group, when it came to the clarifying question section, let go—relaxed—let their guard down and

related in more habitually familiar ways.

In that relaxation, they reverted to old comfortable-slipper ways and thus emerged an old boy banter that included sarcasm, misogyny and descriptive phrases that tended to discourage understanding and encourage self-promotion.

The Clarifying Question section also proves to be the most challenging to

facilitation skills. While enforcement during the first two sections is simple and straight forward, enforcement in the Clarifying Questions section is much more difficult. Often, quick instantaneous judgement calls are asked for. Also complicating the dynamic are emotional reactions to a participant's self-promoting banter.

An example might better illustrate. During a December 2024 session whose theme was Trump's recent election victory, a participant referring to Harris, said the following: "Everyone knows she just spread her legs to get to where she is!". My emotional reaction was instanta-

neous, somatic and intense. I lost control of my breathing and felt a heavy weight on my chest. Somehow, and I really do not know how, I found the ability to stop the conversation and question the statement based on its ability to "encourage understanding." By questioning his word choice and not him or the factual reliability of his statement, I was able to get him to rephrase his statement and move it from self-promoting, misogynist banter to something that asked for understanding. He was able to communicate his belief that she did not obtain her position based on merit.

If any part of the clarifying questions section is successful, it is so because it allows the men to move back to commonality. Often after vulnerable first rounds, in this section, the men move back to joking or reminiscing about what we had in common. Questions and stories about Drake or Des Moines, the Varsity Movie Theatre and of course the fraternity all have a solid grounding effect after the shared vulnerability of the first two rounds.

Are red ones filled with different grains from blue?
Grains of truth in husks of lies.
We must thresh.

Fine grain. Rough grain. Dry grain.
Cracked and sprouting grain.
Wet, rotted grain. Silage.
Digested. Fermented in bags.
In-forming. Shaping who we are

as we grow, age, ingrained in
silos   red   silos   blue.

Media funnels our information,
but we can choose
what fills our silos.

Structure and Enforcement of that Structure:

Structure and the enforcement of that structure can provide the sense of security and the before-mentioned ritual, that is necessary for any meaningful and vulnerable sharing to occur. Facilitators who are willing to enforce the rules, who are willing to call out participants who are not following the agreed upon guidelines, help provide that security. Feedback from our participants consistently thanked us for the structure and our active enforcement of that structure.

Let the Men Speak:

During each year of our group dialogues, we asked the participants for feedback. We sent them a questionnaire and requested they give meaningful thought to their answers. The feedback was extensive, thought out and often very vulnerable. The following is sample of that feedback. Each quote comes from a different participant.

Our black-n-white silo had Walter Cronkite,
Huntley/Brinkley, and Johnnie Carson
    to tell us what was Truth and what was not.
Cronkite made me think Captain Kangaroo
    was behind the news
        because they were both on CBS.
Huntley/Brinkley brought me Beethoven
    with their intro from the Ninth Symphony.
        It took years to separate slashing strings
        and timpani from images of war,
            to uncouple Uncle Walter from the Captain's Puffin' Billie.
        Neither   sorting-out   completed.

Johnnie lived in the dark magic hour
    when I was thought to be in bed, asleep.
Glittering, scary glimpses from a boyish grin,
    watched secretly through a door,
            cracked-open.

- Listening: My ability to listen objectively, with an open mind has improved. It seems to be a learned skill. I find I get much more out of a conversation by listening to what is being said rather than judging the person speaking and preparing a response to what they are saying. Following with questions about how that person came to that belief is the more interesting part of the conversation. This has carried beyond the group.
- The reason someone holds the world view that they do is often based on life events that happened long ago. Knowing and holding that increases my patience when listening to someone express views with which I strongly disagree.
- I became aware from this Zoom group that I view the world through a negative lens and have made many life decisions based on my need to be accepted and valued. I now know I need to get out of my funk by finding ways to volunteer and get more active in my community.
- A number of the group have expressed how much satisfaction they get through volunteer efforts. I have found this to be true and have increased the amount of volunteer work I do with homeless and other community efforts.
- I wonder if people have a true sense of being heard, do they feel genuinely listened to? I tend to think not. Even in the shortest of interactions with people I now want them to feel heard.
- I have re-learned from this experience the importance of being a mindful listener in an attempt to understand before expecting to be understood.

Our Red Silo is safe.
Protected.
We are armed.
Our Red Silo is a smokestack
makes us strong.
We have freedom from fear.

Our Blue Silo is smart.
Well informed.
We know things.
Our Blue Silo's a library
all is taught.
We have freedom to love

- Very little of the group's discussion has been about career accomplishments. A number of members have had great financial success, but the conversations generally center around family and other personal interests. This is reassuring to me because I worked primarily in the public sector and haven't accumulated a lot of financial wealth. My career did allow me to make contributions that I am proud of, but money is not one of those things.
- I've actually experienced from this group what I've known and taught—that people differ in their willingness and/or ability to disclose, even in a relatively safe environment that we've attempted to create.
- People are really different than their beliefs. I have learned how to listen and look for what is underneath or behind views being expressed.

Application of Group Learnings

While our experiment continues via Zoom, my focus and concerns are more local and in person. My concern is that local organizations that can provide the bond of commonality are missing the mark. Churches, civic groups and local university and junior college programs like the Osher Lifelong Learning Institutes are remiss. They are missing an opportunity to play a vital role in bridging our current national cultural divide. They could provide the common ground necessary for the speaking and understanding of difference.

We have learned that the shared commonality that makes possible listening and understanding extremely different world views must be one made from choice. The commonalty that grounds us must be the result of a voluntary choice we have made. Our group had all chosen to attend Drake University and to pledge the same fraternity. That common choice created the bond that made listening to and understanding difficult views possible.

Members of local church groups and civic organizations are members by choice. They have chosen to attend the Baptist church on the corner or to become members of the local Chamber of Commerce. The bond of a common choice can create an atmosphere that allows for the understanding of potentially divisive differences. Several of us have taken on that challenge—to engage local organizations that can provide the commonality that allows for understanding across difference. We are in the process of sharing our learnings, our structure and our enthusiasm.

Concluding Personal Notes

From the Poet:

At our regular meeting, two weeks after the 2024 election, John and I shared our reactions—his in the form of a developing essay, and mine in the form of a poem I had written the day after the election and read to an audience the very next evening. As we shared what we had, we quickly realized that my poem—if expanded to be more than a response from my own silo, but to encompass my understanding of those in their red ones—would integrate well with his essay.

John and I choose excerpts from the resulting poem, and placed selected stanzas within the piece. The original poem, My Blue Silo, appears at the end of this article, and the entire poem, American Silos, can been found here.

OUR BLUE SILO
November 6, 2024

Our blue silo
    has an infinite zenith.
        I can see the edge of the universe from our porch.
    It will take forever to get there, even longer
        with this latest crushing blow
            to the world's collective soul.
                In the meantime,
Our blue silo
    has hot running water,
        a new septic tank with a cute blue cap,
        a garage, driveway, and stainless-steel fridge
            with food and drink from the North Coast Co-op.

        Our power comes from infinity, too—
Our silo's cozy warmth flows from a pump
    driven by twelve black light-drinking panels
        lined up edge to edge on our composite
            tar-shingled roof, glass bodies in the sun,

            our foundation built of other bodies;
    immigrants forced by hands seen and unseen
        hands with weapons, arms of false affection
    bodies lined up head to foot, hip to hip
        in the bellies of banal prison-ships—
            Trafalgar—Hermosa—Guerrero—Brooks,
    bound, brood-bred, gaslit, and sold,
        while others here—as there—and everywhere
            women   children   elders
            Renewing the World
              on Tuluwat Island
            cudgeled in murder-ceremonies
        by the drunken priests of Christ's holy greed
        prancing around the reddening sacred ground
        with whiskey jugs—axes—clubs
            all to a snappy reel of Dixie.

Our Blue Silo also has a view!
    a tube of filtered light—no longer black-n-white—
            that speaks to us,
        watches us watching, hears us listening
        feeds us rations of bull and chicken-shit
        until we're full of it   and empty   blind
        and blinded to the musky star-link cloud
            that streaks across our opening above,
            blurring out stars, a skid-mark on the night,
            deaf and deafened to the distant booming
    fire growing nearer every day.

My inner silo has an exit
    I would rather not use,
        though everyone knows in time they must.
    I tried to escape through the lighted tube
        but was caught in a web of looping roundabouts,
            mocking lemniscates,
        that brought me back to terminal, digital comfort.
Desperate to be nearer to the zenith, I climbed the walls
    but got no closer to the sky.
              I fell.
        Thank you, love,
        for bringing me back home.

This time I'll keep my eyes on the zenith,
    close them when the star-link monster screams,
    fix my heart-mind on the starry circle,
    and sing full-voiced so my song might make it out,
        soft to you of love, and of our children
        in their greener
        more transparent
            silos in the sun
        and hope to share this place without complacence
            through all the time we may still have as one.
      ~   ~   ~

From the essayist:

How long our group continues to dialogue is a mystery. We are getting older. People will die.

Somehow, for each of us, the process of aging has benefitted from our continued attempts at understanding each other. I think aging, as a process, responds to and values the attempt.

The dialogue session we had immediately following the November election was by far the most difficult for me, and yes, I did write a column about that difficulty. The election results caused me to question all that I hold dear and identify with. I identified as someone who thought he knew what was going on. I was wrong. So wrong! How could my perceptions of reality have been so mistaken. I tried but failed to communicate that during the first dialogue after the election. The election was a binary choice. There were winners and losers. For more than three years now we have been working on breaking down the binary, searching for the crack in between, the one where the light comes in. Yes, I find great comfort in Leonard Cohen; but here we were faced with the starkest of binaries. It was difficult. But we continue, we continue to listen and speak for understanding. Our aging process benefits from the attempt.

Over the years I have learned the joys of letting myself discover the self-reflective journey that can be writing. Writing with a desire to communicate. I have attempted to do so here. I cannot, like my father, be part of two grotesquely different world views walking home in silence, neither questioning the other until many decades later.

Dovelion: A Fairy Tale for our Times

Eileen R. Tabios

Review by Glenn Aparicio Parry

"Once upon a time, standing in front of a grey building, pushing the button to Apartment 3J," this immensely important novel begins/was written/and maybe never ends. A richly complicated and timeless glimpse into the fairy tale we call modernity, Dovelion (Duh-vee-li-on) defies easy description. It begins like a somewhat kinky love story, with two passionate lovers, one woman and and one gender fluid person, one the more submissive mentee and the other the more dominant mentor, brought together in such a unique and convoluted manner that it takes the entire book to reveal the depth of their interconnectedness. But Dovelion is not a love story, at least not only. Neither is it only a story of personal redemption, a political drama, suspense story, poetry, prose, fact or fiction—although it is all of that and more. Reality, to paraphrase Walt Whitman, 'contains multitudes.' Reality is large enough to contain poetry, prose, fact, fiction, magic, imagination, passion,

Glenn Aparicio Parry, is a Nautilus award-winning author of *Original Thinking: A Radical Revisioning of Time, Humanity, and Nature* (North Atlantic Press, 2015), *Original Politics: Making America Sacred Again* (SelectBooks, 2020), the first two thirds of the trilogy that preceded *Original Love: The Timeless Source of Wholeness* (Select Books, 2026).

revenge, justice, and more. Ultimately, reality is large enough to contain even fairy tales. And that only begins to give the reader an inkling of what Dovelion is all about.

To understand Dovelion, you almost need a soundtrack, for the one thing that is constant about Dovelion is its rhythm. Herbie Hancock's Chameleon Man would do nicely. It begins with a repeating beat: Badomp ba domp domp domp, badomp ba domp ba domp and just when you are hypnotized by the repeating phrasing, it gradually, surreptitiously, changes and expands with a myriad of cascading variations on the theme. Suddenly, you realize you are in completely new territory, even after you return to the original beat. The author employs the same device in Dovelion. Over and over again, we hear "Once upon a time, standing in front of a grey building…" and "Once upon a time, an emerald island laid upon a blue, sapphire ocean…"and "Once upon a time, I thought poetry was a fairy tale…" and then slowly are shifted out of that reality. By the end, the grey building is no longer grey and the poetry is no longer a fairy tale, but a gripping reality, a suspenseful political thriller, a murder mystery, a search for one's roots, and a visit from one's ancestors. The novel unfolds like a kaleidoscope of fractals; it

is deeply rooted, like a large tree; it has rings inside its bark, but its energy also expands outward, radiating and reaching out to connect with other trees and with the whole cosmos. The overall effect is one of exploration into a richly textured, interconnected, multidimensional universe. The layers are revealed one by one, until in the end, we glimpse the whole.

The breath of the philosophical themes in Dovelion are too varied and expansive to cover in a brief review—but the main point the author always returns to is how everything is interconnected and interrelated across time and space. Tabios calls this *Kapwa time.* There is no past, no present, no future as we normally think of them in Kapwa time. The past, present, and future exist simultaneously; any event that has occurred continues to exist somewhere in spacetime. Kapwa time includes everything, including what in the normal world we would call contradictions. "Once upon a time, I wake up and I am old that day." But I am the same me that was young. Once upon a time, I am in a love affair, and even after my lover dies, they are still there. The only difficulty with Kapwa time is that pain never disappears. Everything is as fresh as the moment it occurred. The upside is that there is always enough time. Even when her lover dies, the time between them was sufficient.

I hesitate to say too much of the plot other than the bare bones, lest it be misconstrued. Elena, the main protagonist, is the daughter of someone ordered to be killed by the father of they, Ernst, her gender fluid lover who was the son of a CIA agent. Elena's father was killed by a dictator in Pacifica, a made-up country close to the Philippines in more ways than one; her mother was a rising political star supported by the CIA who died giving birth to our protagonist, or so we are told. The facts and the truth become malleable in this story, just like the time. How the son of a dictator's supporter and the orphan daughter of the father murdered by the same dictator could meet, let alone become lovers, is explainable only by the fact that in Kapwa time, everything is related and everything is part of each other. Nonetheless, there is great tension in the plot due to the odd juxtaposition of the participants. There is an overarching sense of fate pervading the story, not unlike the great Greek myths or tragedies.

Dovelion reads like an ancient myth, and like the great myths, the energy of the past continues to live in the present. As the plot unfolds, and more and more details are revealed, Gibran's words ring in my ears. "Your joy is your sorrow unmasked."[1] The inverse relationship between joy and sorrow is evident throughout the story. It is through reaching deep into her wounds that she finds her salvation. It is in the confronting of pain, not the running away from it, that she learns the truth of her life. When her lover dies, the building is no longer grey. "There is no longer any need to miss you," she realizes. "We are all one."

To be an orphan is to live in an alternative universe, but that too is interconnected with the normative universe. Her struggle to find out the truth about her mother, whether her father ever loved her, is all revealed in due course. The protagonist, like the author, is a poet. Clearly, the author's purpose in writing this was not to write poetry, but to find a better life.

In the end, she learns she was not who she thought she was. And that is her saving grace.

She discovers that her heritage and poetry are for a purpose. She discovers her words are healing, that her poetry can change the world. Most importantly, she discovers herself. "It is never too late to have a happy childhood," wrote Tom Robbins at the end of *Still Life of a Woodpecker.*[2] The same could be said about Dovelion. In Kapwa time, it is possible to live happily ever after. It may require being in a liminal, metaphoric space, but it is possible to exist ever after in the bosom of one's ancestors. In truth, those ancestors have been with us all along, supporting and inspiring us. The veil between life and death is thinner than we realize. They are as interconnected as the roots and branches of a tree.

In the end, Dovelion is a book about love, for it is love that interconnects us together, that makes us all one with each other across time, with our friends, lovers, enemies, ancestors, and the yet to be born. In this sense, Dovelion is a love story after all. "You should bring the past into the future, through love," says Elena. And indeed, she does. This fluidity of reality is what makes Dovelion a true fairy tale for our times. And that is quite the accomplishment.

Endnotes

[1] Gibran, Kahlil. *The Prophet.* New York. (1973), p. 29.

[2] Robbins, Tom. *Still Life with Woodpecker.* New York. Bantam, (1990), p. 277.

The Encounter
by Chun Yu

Every encounter with a flower
Is a blessing

The flower blossoms toward me
I blossom toward the flower
Who is blossoming?

Every encounter in the world
Is an encounter of the self

A flower's beauty
Gives me the courage to see

I see all things
All things see me

All is
I am

The Mystical Exodus in Jungian Perspective: Transforming Trauma and the Wellspring of Renewal

Shoshana Fershtman. New York; Routledge:, 2021. 268 pages. $155.00 cloth; $38.95 pa-per; $35.05 VitalSource e-book.

Review by Lisa Herman, Ph.D., MFT, REAT

Shoshana Fershtman significantly contributes to the canon interpreting the Jews' miraculous escape from slavery in Egypt. The Mystical Exodus is a much-needed feminine interpretation. The story is situated in the zeitgeist of our times of transformation and the tradition of Passover when the old story is told in the present. Dr. Fershtman in her multi-threaded narrative offers a way to psychologically recover from the trauma of slavery, historical and personal - a daunting task that she executes with remarkable skill. This complex storybook, a heavily referenced inquiry into the rediscovery of the Divine Feminine, is complimented by interviews with those carrying the burdens and joy of our ancestors informed by a Jungian analysis. Dr. Fershtman presents her case claiming that the Divine Feminine as a spiritual and socially conscious force ensures the survival of the Jewish people.

One of many threads weaving through the Mystical Exodus is the original story with Fershtman's reading of them Joseph

Lisa Herman, Ph.D., MFT, REAT, Independent Scholar. Lisa is an expressive arts therapist, associate professor at N. California grad schools, writer, and actor.

in Egypt and his bones, Lilith as Shadow at the Red Sea are only a few of these. The Kabbala's interpretation of the ten Plagues as related to the ten Sephirot, the role of the Matriarchs and many dreams and legends also appear. As Fershtman also offers moving soulful histories of interviewees who found a home for their spiritual longing in 'Jewish Renewal', a movement rooted in Northern California, these so many multi-colored strands sometimes become hard to untangle.

Jews returning to Judaism is one thread. After being disillusioned with their post-Holocaust parents' practices of striving for the trappings of success in America, money, and power, or joining social movements aimed at egalitarian societies where everyone belonged without the stumbling block of religion, they felt how Spirit was missing from parents' solutions. Fershtman situates parents' choices as coping mechanisms originating from historical trauma and describes our forebears with compassionate understanding. the book These

next-generation disenchanted Jews had a dream, a breakthrough moment and found the light through now an established branch of Judaism called 'Jewish Renewal'.

Fershtman's personal narrative begins in the 60's when many of us sought new ways for being and relating. We

rejected the constrictions of the previous generation and eschewed the dire consequences of its thinking. We made our own music, loved who we wanted and challenged structures that inhibited our evolution. We found our tribes and danced and cooked together. We wrote poems of resistance and peace and struggle. In those embodied days of alternative ways to inhabit the world, we were exposed to Eastern ways of being, drug induced epiphanies of Oneness with the planet and Something Else, as well as solutions for our dis-ease. Rabbi Zalman Schachter-Shalomi an emigrant from Vienna brought the Hassidic tradition morphed into Jewish Renewal as his solution. He preached this Judaism, more joyous than somber, in America and fired up a 'Jewish Renewal' for certain young people searching a spiritual connection specific to their heritage.

A lifetime learner of Jewish mysticism Fershtman narrates her personal search through various Californian ways of being and how she finds her mystical tribe in this new movement, now a worldwide organization under the brand ALEPH (The Alliance for Jewish Renewal). Fershtman, also an attorney-at-law, is skillful referring to the past as relevant precedent for the present and the future. She is as deft as any rabbinical scholar reading the Old Testament as evidence for her argument and joins a lineage of sages beginning before the 1st millennium and lasting until now. Many major religions refer to the Bible. Christians read the 'Old Testament' as is a prediction for the coming of Jesus the Messiah. and the Quran for Muslims is read referencing Moses and the Israelites as their ancestors. The Jews read the 'Tanach' 'Old Testament) as our personal biography and spiritual connect to the Divine who chose us to receive it.

Hermeneutic inquiries in studies of intertextuality, find the lacunae in these wisdom books are often where the juice is. For Jewish Renewal the lacuna is the story of the Divine Feminine or in Hebrew the Shekhena. Fershtman argues She was deliberately omitted for survival reasons following Schachter-Shalomi who taught the spiritual elements in Judaism were omitted during the period of the 'Enlightenment' when Logos ruled and ironically Jews wanted to fit in with other religious masculine norms and the ineffable God became a He. Now the replenishing of the spiritual must be renewed so Spirit can provide information vital to us today. Fershtman as an attorney and Jungian analyst is perfectly suited to offer a cogent argument based on her own culture's historical precedent for reinterpreting the Exodus as both a spiritual and healing image relevant to now.

Fershtman's interpretation through a feminine gaze honors Shekhena interspersed throughout the book as the Feminine Presence. Fershtman allows the women of the Exodus - courageous, wise, sexy, dancing and singing women - to lead us out of slavery, through the churning waters into the desert where we produced a new generation who could enter the Promised Land. The story goes how our great, great etc. grandmothers led the people side by side with Moses (Fershtman says he symbolizes the 'Masculine') and sometimes in front of him we claimed our place in the leadership of these sometimes reluctant followers. This Exodus is also a metaphor for how we heal ourselves. We were slaves in Egypt, and we suffered. We lost hope and found it again. We trusted our leaders and then betrayed them. And we kept on moving when our faith was restored. We knew Spirit in our bod-

ies and the evidence before our eyes. Fershtman's and referenced others' psychological interpretations provide the most delightful reading in the book. Tales from the Mishna (originally a record of the oral tradition for everyday guidance from around the beginning of the Common Era and still being written) are a gift to bolster her case. Jewish Renewal as Fershtman argues is a movement that harkens back to when we were immersed in embodied spiritual realms and what we lost in trauma-informed Jewish patriarchal dogma.

She presents our Ashkenazi (Eastern European rooted) parents as handed down a restrictive Judaism by their parents with no heartfelt experience of being a Jew. Fershtman tells us either our parents or grandparents lost at least one relative in the Shoah even if they didn't have knowledge of it. Trauma is in our 'collective unconscious' as Jews. Mom and Dad carried the burden as do we and our children. And before that our back-in-the-day relatives experienced pogroms (a Slavic word originally describing massacres of Jews and their villages in the 19th and 20th century and recently back in the news about actions by whites against blacks in Tulsa.) and we carry that too.

Fershtman's archetypal view links recovery from trauma and the Exodus through stages: leaving the constrictions of Egypt, (the trauma), the fear of moving into unknown dangerous territory (the Red Sea), necessary wandering in the desert when old ways of doing and being are being shed as new selves (babies) emerge and entering the Promised Land (connection with the Divine). Particularly eye-catching is the phrase we need to banish our 'inner Pharaoh', the restrictive Protector (from Kalshead), in order to 'leave Egypt'. She offers how therapeutically we need nourishment during the reconstruction time in our sand dunes equating this period with the experience of the Jews being nurtured by God the manna-giver and the Shekinah our water-provider, and getting directional guidance (a therapist?) From those magical/natural GPS's of cloud and fire

that appear like magic.

The Divine Feminine has been lost, shrouded to hide her sexuality and creative playfulness and we lost through her our connection to the Divine. The Shekhena closeted behind closed doors as she was in many religions was given prohibitions so she wouldn't run amok. Fershtman with compassion presents the case why we needed rigidity and respect for Laws and Order and the reasons our great great) grandparents sought a codified route to ironically fit in with their contemporaries. Fershtman as historian is convincing, we weren't always so restrictive on ourselves. And that takes us back to the title story and the Mystical Psychological Social Exodus from slavery and our time to reset and renew.

Fershtman concludes by recommending we continue to interpret the 'Torah' of old beliefs as well as previous codified interpretations. We need to ask questions and question those who don't want us to ask. What's the point of being human if we don't debate our multifaceted bibles? They say you can't have two Jews with the same opinion. We are the people who ask why. Fershtman's book invites us to delve deeper into our disagreements. Is this our light unto the nations?

M.A. Programme in Indigenous Science and Peace Studies

Is it for you?

Do you want to solve today's global crises facing humanity by transforming outdated paradigms?

Are you inspired to learn how Indigenous knowledge and Western science can be employed across disciplines and professions to transform crises and conflicts, and build peace?

Do you want to spend a year studying in an academically challenging environment, at a global university with students, faculty, and Indigenous Elders drawn from around the world?

What will you learn?

Steeped in Indigenous Knowledge Systems and methodologies, the Master's degree in Indigenous Science and Peace Studies (ISPS) will train you to be an insightful and self-reflective researcher and practitioner who understands central epistemological, ontological, and ethical issues that impact diplomacy, policymaking, and community work. You will become a reflexive communicator, trained to transform the global development field in ways that align our future societies with the values and resources rooted in the earth. Through this programme, you will obtain:

- A synthesis of indigenous scientific research and theory relevant to the transformation of conflicts and current development paradigm, as well as a diversity of perspectives that impact peace, justice, security, sovereignty, and reconciliation.
- Detailed knowledge of the United Nations System and related institutions, procedures and instruments that affect decision-making regarding Indigenous peoples and traditional knowledge relevant for work in the field.
- Skills and practices for effective scholarship honoring both Indigenous ways of knowing and emergent Western sciences; profound self-reflections as part of a renewed understanding of self and identity; and policy formulation, peacebuilding and humanitarian work.
- Knowing who you are in your complex cultural and ethnic identity, understanding the place and history of where you live and work, and understanding the integrative power of holistic and transrational processes (such as dreams and visions) is part of the programme. This process provides a unique framework and educational foundation to explore and resolve some of the world's most critical problems. It enables students to become more effective policymakers, community workers, diplomats, activists, and communicators who create change to renew life on earth.

M.A. in Indigenous Science and Peace: University-wide Courses

You will receive, along with your peers from other programmes, courses on Peace and Conflict theories and practices, the UN system, the relationship of identity politics and peacebuilding, and research methods. The students of this M.A. programme will also receive practical training on working in conflict areas. For more information about these courses and the program in general, see https://isri.wisn.org.

M.A. in Indigenous Science and Peace: Programme-specific Courses

In addition to the university-wide courses, students in this programme will take programme-specific courses.

- Ethnoautobiographical Inquiry - Ancestral and Historical Research 1

- Bridging Paradigms – The Role of Dreams and Dreaming

- Indigenous Knowledge & Research Methodologies

- Colonial History, Decoloniality, & Sovereignty Indigenous Science Methods

- Ethnoautobiographical Inquiry - Ancestral and Historical Research 2

- Representing Indigenous Mind – Decolonial Representation in Publications and Media

- The Science of Archaeoastronomy & Indigenous Star Knowledge

- Interventions – Capstone Project Preparation Model UN Conference: Committee on Indigenous Rights

- Thesis/Capstone/Internship